T0311907

POWER

Power plays a central role in business and management. But what is power exactly, and what are key elements of this concept? Defining power as relative ability, this book discusses structures of power, individual power, the exercise of power, strategy, and collective power.

While discussing these key components, ideas of important thinkers about power, from Plato to Foucault, Weber to Lukes, Machiavelli to Kahneman, Sun to Kotter, and Barnard to Clegg, are discussed and interpretively categorized into a toolbox of conceptual elements – what Blumer referred to as sensitizing concepts. This toolbox of sensitizing concepts allows the selection of those elements of the concept of power that provide the most constructive and effective practical understanding in particular situations.

The core message behind the discussion is that knowledge of key components of the concept of power is empowering. It is empowering to learn about aspects of structures of power, individual power, the exercise of power, strategy, and collective power. Understanding such conceptual components empowers students, researchers, practitioners, and other readers to use their understanding in interpreting, theorizing about, and dealing with the complexities of power in their particular situations – without tying them to any preconceived general theories about power.

Reinoud Bosch, PhD, is an independent academic with a background in technical computer science, economics, and political and social sciences. He has held positions at and performed assignments for Nyenrode Business University, the University of Amsterdam Business School, the Royal Netherlands Academy of Arts and Sciences, Rotterdam School of Management at Erasmus University, and the European University Institute.

Key Ideas in Business and Management
Edited by **Stewart Clegg**

Understanding how business affects and is affected by the wider world is a challenge made more difficult by the disaggregation between various disciplines, from operations research to corporate governance. This series features concise books that break out from disciplinary silos to facilitate understanding by analysing key ideas that shape and influence business, organizations, and management.

Each book focuses on a key idea, locating it in relation to other fields, facilitating deeper understanding of its applications and meanings, and providing critical discussion of the contribution of relevant authors and thinkers. The books provide students and scholars with thought-provoking insights that aid the study and research of business and management.

Sustainability
A Key Idea for Business and Society
Suzanne Benn, Melissa Edwards and Tim Williams

Human Rights
A Key Idea for Business and Society
Karin Buhmann

Complexity
A Key Idea for Business and Society
Chris Mowles

Power
A Key Idea for Business and Society
Reinoud Bosch

For more information about this series, please visit: www.routledge.com/Key-Ideas-in-Business-and-Management/book-series/KEYBUS

POWER

A Key Idea for Business and Society

Reinoud Bosch

LONDON AND NEW YORK

Cover image: NeoLeo / Getty images

First published 2022
by Routledge
2 Park Square, Milton Park, Abingdon, Oxon OX14 4RN

and by Routledge
605 Third Avenue, New York, NY 10158

Routledge is an imprint of the Taylor & Francis Group, an informa business

British Library Cataloguing-in-Publication Data
A catalogue record for this book is available from the British Library

Library of Congress Cataloging-in-Publication Data
Library of Congress Cataloging-in-Publication Data
Names: Bosch, Reinoud, author.
Title: Power : a key idea for business and society / Reinoud Bosch.
Description: Abingdon, Oxon ; New York, NY : Routledge, 2022. |
Series: Key ideas in business and management | Includes bibliographical
references and index.
Identifiers: LCCN 2021039487 (print) | LCCN 2021039488 (ebook)
Subjects: LCSH: Power (Social sciences)
Classification: LCC HN49.P6 B673 2022 (print) | LCC HN49.P6
(ebook) | DDC 303.3—dc23
LC record available at https://lccn.loc.gov/2021039487
LC ebook record available at https://lccn.loc.gov/2021039488

ISBN: 978-0-367-47197-2 (hbk)
ISBN: 978-0-367-45645-0 (pbk)
ISBN: 978-1-003-03410-0 (ebk)

DOI: 10.4324/9781003034100

Typeset in Bembo
by codeMantra

CONTENTS

ACKNOWLEDGMENTS

Back in 1986, when I was a computer science undergraduate at the Amsterdam University of Applied Sciences, I had the opportunity to spend an internship in a company in Taipei, Taiwan. I became intrigued by the Chinese attitude to work–life, which struck me as rather different from what I was used to in my home country, the Netherlands. This Chinese attitude to work–life appeared to have a stimulating effect on economic development, an idea which was at the time referred to as the hypothesis of the 'Confucian ethic' (Kahn, 1979). After receiving my computer science degree, I decided to stay intrigued and embarked on an economics study at the University of Amsterdam to see what I could learn about this hypothesis. But unfortunately, the main economic textbooks of the time did not discuss this hypothesis at all. Instead, they were mostly concerned with applying the model of the 'rational actor' – that "lightning calculator of pleasures and pains, who oscillates like a homogenous globule of desires and happiness under the impulse of stimuli that shift him about the area, but leave him intact" (Veblen, 1898, p. 389). Fortunately, for a computer scientist, the 'technical' part of economics was not very challenging, and so I was able to spend lots of time in philosophy, psychology, sociology, anthropology, and political science libraries, to see what a more realistic approach to understanding the economy could look like. This was when I had the fortune of meeting the late Jos de Beus, who pointed me to important literature on philosophy of science, cross-cultural psychology, social theory, politics, and ethics. It slowly dawned upon me that for a realistic approach to economics, the following elements were needed: a convincing basis in the philosophy of science; a clear methodology; a thorough understanding of basic social theory; attention to psychology, culture, and organization; and, most importantly, a central position for the concept of power.

With these ideas in mind, I pursued a PhD in political and social sciences at the European University Institute in Florence, Italy. There, I had the great pleasure of meeting Arpad Szakolczai who provided me with a thorough introduction into interpretive methodology, Steven Lukes who had just written an instructive seminar paper on power, the late Isabella Matauschek and Uta Gerhardt who introduced me to systematic Weberian-hermeneutical methodology, and Gianfranco Poggi who was working on his book *Forms of Power* (2001). Using a Weberian-hermeneutical methodology was not generally accepted at the EUI, and I am infinitely grateful to have been supported in my application of this methodology by Peter Wagner. I also received important support from Bo Stråth and from encounters with Tom Heller, Neil Fligstein, and Amitai Etzioni, for which I remain grateful.

A next impetus to writing this book came from Hennie Boeije, who was kind enough to invite me to be a co-author of an article on the philosophy of science for qualitative research. Through Hennie, I came into contact with Boom Uitgevers where, with the much appreciated support of Joris Bekkers and Selma Hoedt, I published a book on philosophy of science for qualitative research as well as an earlier book on power. In an attempt to instigate a discussion on power in the Dutch qualitative research journal *KWALON* for which I was coordinating editor-in-chief, I sent a copy of my earlier book to Stewart Clegg. Rather to my surprise, Stewart invited me to write a new book on power for this series on key ideas for business and society. I am most grateful to Stewart for providing me with this opportunity.

As was to be expected, writing this book was a solitary process. As the independent academic I have turned out to be, I am grateful to have had the opportunity to work as a management thesis advisor and evaluator for the University of Amsterdam Business School and Nyenrode Business University. I have particularly enjoyed the constructive and wide-ranging multi-disciplinary nature of this work and my positive contacts with both students and faculty – even if many recent contacts had to occur online due to the Covid-19 pandemic. Having reinvigorated my IT knowledge in recent years, I have also become a tester and mentor at deeplearning.ai, which has provided me with similar constructive and positive online experiences with co-workers and learners, and which has given me important insights into the facts and fictions of data science and artificial intelligence.

Many thanks are due to Terry Clague at Routledge for his patience and continuing support. I also owe much gratitude to Hester Elzerman for love and support. My son Vincent kept me on edge, by forcing me to try to defend myself against the fried liver attack in chess, sending me explanations of the working of quantum computers, and by simply being there and showing me the bright side of things. It has been a long intellectual journey since my encounter with the idea of the 'Confucian ethic' back in 1986. This book presents the analysis of power I have ended up with. May it empower you.

REFERENCES

Kahn, H. (1979). *World economic development: 1979 and beyond*. Boulder, CO: Westview Press.

Poggi, G. (2001). *Forms of power*. Cambridge: Polity.

Veblen, T. (1898). Why is economics not an evolutionary science? *Quarterly Journal of Economics, 12*(4), 373–397. https://doi.org/10.2307/1882952.

INTRODUCTION

When Frederick the Great, King of Prussia, read Machiavelli's political treatise *The Prince*, he expressed repugnance. In the foreword to his essay *Anti-Machiavel*, he wrote:

> I will defend humanity against this monster which wants to destroy it.
>
> *(Frederick the Great, 1740)*

His argument against *The Prince* was a moral one:

> I always have regarded The Prince as one of the most dangerous works which were spread in the world; it is a book which falls naturally into the hands of princes, and of those who have a taste for policy. It is all too easy for an ambitious young man, whose heart and judgement are not formed enough to accurately distinguish good from bad, to be corrupted by maxims which inflame his hunger for power.
>
> *(ibid.)*

What might it have been about *The Prince* that made Frederick the Great write these words?

For one, *The Prince* focuses on actual workings of power rather than morality. In *The Prince*, if power is at stake, moral issues lose out. Second, *The Prince* was presented as a gift to Lorenzo de' Medici, then ruler of Florence. It was written as advice to someone who wants to attain or retain power, and it prescribes not to remain moral in those instances where such is required to stay in power:

DOI: 10.4324/9781003034100-1

> if a ruler wants to survive, he'll have to learn to stop being good, at least
> when the occasion demands.
>
> *(Machiavelli, 1532/2009, p. 60)*

A good example of how the wish to attain and retain power may supersede morality is provided by Frederick the Great himself. As Blanning puts it in his biography of the Prussian ruler:

> he took the decision to seize the Austrian province of Silesia. To put it
> simply, he began by robbing an apparently defensive woman and spent the
> rest of his life trying to hang on to his booty.
>
> *(Blanning, 2016, p. 32)*

Importantly, *The Prince* does not hide ideas about the workings of power, repugnant as they may be, but makes them available to an audience. The ideas used by Frederick the Great to attain and retain his power over his subjects are less obvious, but his self-ascription of morality undoubtedly was one – and perfectly consistent with the prescription of *The Prince* for a ruler to seem virtuous (Machiavelli, 1532/2009, pp. 60–61). If Frederick the Great were really such a moral person, why did he retain the absolute power he held?

In fact, as argued by Galbraith (1983, p. 141), is it not the best service to power to cultivate the belief that it does not exist? And, if this argument is turned upside-down, is it then not the worst service to power to show that it exists and to describe how it works? Should *The Prince*, considered from that perspective, not be seen as a moral work rather than a dangerous one? And, are absolutist rulers claiming to be moral, such as Frederick the Great, not the dangerous ones?

This debate on the moral nature of *The Prince* is an old one, and the morality of the book has been defended by various authors through time (Benner, 2009, 2013; Scott, 2016). But the question whether a book about power should attempt to describe the actual workings of power, amoral as they may be, or whether it should restrict itself in one way or another to moral usages of power remains an important one. After all, a clear description of the nature and the workings of power provides those with an inclination to abuse it with the knowledge of how to do so effectively. As a case in point, according to Rees (2004), both Mussolini and Stalin read *The Prince*, providing some indication of the type of audience that may be attracted to this kind of explicit expositions of the workings of power. At the same time, moral prescriptions of some kind can easily be abused as well, as demonstrated by the example of Frederick the Great. This also holds for utopian visions, which may and have been used to legitimate and facilitate genocide (Clegg et al., 2012).

The position taken in this book is that exposing the concept and workings of power as much and as clearly as possible to anyone willing to read about it may, in fact, decrease the possibilities for power abuse and support the constructive use of power. In other words, publicly providing knowledge about power, no matter how repugnant, is seen as *empowering*. If only absolutist rulers, such as Frederick the Great, have knowledge of the workings of power, it is easy for them to abuse their power. In contrast, if many people know how power works, it may be much more difficult for absolutist rulers to abuse power, or, indeed, to become absolutist rulers in the first place. Instead, the best way to use power in a situation where many people know how it works may well be to use it constructively, possibly in cooperation with, but at least not abusive of others. Interestingly, this position is in line with the argument proposed by Montesquieu, fierce critic of Machiavelli, that power must check power (Montesquieu, 1748/1989, p. 155; Sullivan, 2017). It is also in line with Benner's (2009) argument that Machiavelli's ethics is one of self-legislation by citizens.

This is by no means to imply that the position taken in this book is sufficient from a moral perspective. It is clear that a wide-reaching ethical debate about the workings of power remains of overwhelming importance. It is important to recognize though that ethical arguments and systems are prone to be abused. This is why an exposition of the workings of power is essential to any authentic and constructive ethical discussion.

Up to this point, *The Prince* has served as a figurehead in the discussion about whether or not ideas about the workings of power should be made public as much as possible. Other publications that could have served this purpose are, for instance, Sun's *The Art of War* (6th cent. BC/1971) or, more challengingly, Von Clausewitz's *On War* (1832/1989). But a general book concerned with public or business administration could also have served this purpose. Many books about administration are concerned with the workings of power in one way or another, whether they address governance, strategy, change management, marketing, finance, public relations, human resource management, or organizational behavior. It is not a coincidence that ideas derived from *The Prince*, *The Art of War*, and *On War* have been proposed for business (McNeilly, 1996; Brennan, 2015; Paley, 2015). If power is central to society, it is central to business. The position taken in this book is that providing knowledge about how power works may lead to more constructive, empowering uses of power in business and less abuse of power.

Now, power comes in many guises. In this book, these are presented in the form of different categories of power: structures of power, individual power, exercising power, strategy, and collective power. These different categories are all elements of the concept of power in a general sense, but they have differences in meaning and constitution – as will become clear when these categories are discussed in subsequent chapters.

Importantly, the perspective taken in this book is processual. In social life, power and its manifestations are never completely stable, and this should be accounted for by the way in which power is discussed. Important elements in this discussion are the meanings of such social phenomena often referred to as 'structures' or 'institutions'. In this book, the term 'structure' is used to refer to relationships. In line with Weber's (1922/1978) definition of relationship, relationships can be seen as possibilities of certain types of interactions taking place.

Such possibilities are never completely stable. The same holds for rules and regulations, which always depend on ever-changing interpretations. Other phenomena sometimes referred to as 'institutions' are similarly non-stable, such as habits, patterns of actions, or the concept of mental structures which is so central to individual power.

Power, then, has the potential to be abused. But the more people know about it, and the more people understand what power consists of and how it works, the lower the chances may be for anyone to abuse power based on superior knowledge about power. And because power is never stable, there is no stable basis for those wishing to abuse power. Instead, spreading knowledge about power may empower those who learn about it, so that power may be used constructively. But first: what *is* power?

References

Benner, E. (2009). *Machiavelli's ethics*. Princeton, NJ: Princeton University Press.

Benner, E. (2013). *Machiavelli's prince: A new reading*. Oxford: Oxford University Press.

Blanning, T. (2016). *Frederick the Great: King of Prussia*. New York: Random House.

Brennan, S. (2015). *Machiavelli on business: Strategies, advice, and words of wisdom on business and power*. New York: Skyhorse Publishing.

Clegg, S., Pina e Cunha, M., & Rego, A. (2012). The theory and practice of utopia in a total institution: The pineapple panopticon. *Organization Studies*, *33*(12), 1735–1757. https://doi.org/10.1177/0170840612464611.

Frederick the Great (1740). *Anti-Machiavel*. Retrieved 1 December 2020, from https://archive.org/download/AntiMachiavelFrederickstheGreat/Anti-Machiavel%20-%20 Friedrich%20II%20Hohenzollern.pdf.

Galbraith, J.K. (1983). *The anatomy of power*. Boston, MA: Houghton Mifflin.

Machiavelli, N. (1532/2009). *The prince* (T. Parks, Trans.). London: Penguin Books.

McNeilly, M. (1996). *Sun Tzu and the art of business: Six strategic principles for managers*. Oxford: Oxford University Press.

Montesquieu (1748/1989). *The spirit of the laws* (A.M. Cohler, B.C. Miller, & H.S. Stone, Eds.). Cambridge: Cambridge University Press.

Paley, N. (2015). *Clausewitz talks business. An executive's guide to thinking like a strategist*. Boca Raton, FL: CRC Press.

Rees, E.A. (2004). *Political thought from Machiavelli to Stalin: Revolutionary Machiavellism*. Houndmills: Palgrave Macmillan.

Scott, J.T. (2016). *The Routledge guidebook to Machiavelli's: The prince*. London: Routledge.

Sullivan, V.B. (2017). *Montesquieu & the despotic ideas of Europe: An interpretation of the spirit of the laws*. Chicago, IL: The University of Chicago Press.

Sun (6th cent. BC/1971). *The art of war* (S.B. Griffith, Trans.). Oxford: Oxford University Press.

Von Clausewitz, C. (1832/1989). *On war* (M. Howard & P. Paret, Eds. & Trans.). Princeton, NJ: Princeton University Press.

Weber, M. (1922/1978). *Economy and society* (G. Roth & C. Wittich, Eds.). Berkeley: University of California Press.

1

WHAT IS POWER?

The meaning of the word 'power' has been highly contested. For some, it has negative connotations due to the possibility of its abusive exercise. Others consider the positive role power may play in various forms of agency allowing for individual and collective achievements. In light of this, it is reasonable to argue that power may be viewed negatively or positively depending on the circumstances, the way it is used, and the perspective from which it is considered. This leaves open the question what the word 'power' may be taken to refer to and how we could think of the realm of ideas that is invoked by its use. Historically, various positions have been taken in this regard. A number of these positions will be critically discussed in this chapter, as well as a number of contemporary positions. At the end of the chapter, the reasoned choice is made to define power as relative ability – a definition that aims to empower by providing clarity and understanding.

Historical notions of power

An early definition of power can be found in Plato's *Sophist* (360 BC):

> My notion would be, that anything which possesses any sort of power to affect another, or to be affected by another…has real existence; and I hold that the definition of being is simply power of.

In other words, according to this definition, being – everything that exists – is 'power of'. There is something counterintuitive to this very broad definition. It seems reasonable to argue that everything that exists has a certain power. The earth can be said to have the power to draw objects to its surface through gravity,

DOI: 10.4324/9781003034100-2

a human being can have the power to speak. But that does not equate the earth or a human being to 'power of'. Power rather seems to be something that the earth or a human being can be said to have.

This more intuitive idea of power as something that one can have shows up in the definition of power in Hobbes' *Leviathan* (1651/1996, p. 66):

> The Power *of a man*, (to take it Universally), is his present means, to obtain some future apparent Good.

Here, power is equated to means. According to Hobbes, this includes such things as faculties of body or mind, riches, reputation, friends, good luck, servants, success, the sciences, and instruments of war. While more intuitive, it seems odd to equate power to means. Instead, it seems more reasonable to argue that means enhance power, and that power itself is something else, something that is enabled by means – an ability.

A definition of power as an ability appears in Locke's *An Essay Concerning Human Understanding* (1690/1999, p. 218):

> Power thus considered is two-fold, viz. as able to make, or able to receive any change.

This definition combines the idea of power as an ability with what the effects of this ability may be – a change made or received. As argued above, considering power to be an ability feels intuitively right, but the effects of power would appear to be broader than just making or receiving. They would also seem to include such effects as influencing or feeling. Nonetheless, as will become apparent, Locke's definition has been reinvoked by a popular contemporary definition of power.

There remains the question where this particular ability that power consists of is located. Is it a characteristic of something or someone, or should it be seen as relative to the context? The importance of the context shows up in a popular definition of power proposed by Weber in *Economy and Society* (1922/1978, p. 53):

> "Power" (*Macht*) is the probability that one actor within a social relationship will be in a position to carry out his own will despite resistance, regardless of the basis on which this probability rests.

Here, the notions of social relationship, position, and resistance indicate that power should be seen as relative to a context. Weber defines power as a probability, which is characteristic of his methodological focus on the interpretation of social life in terms of probabilities of social actions. Looked at from a substantive rather than a methodological perspective, Weber's use of the term 'basis' may be taken to refer to the ability discussed earlier. Notable in Weber's definition is the attention it pays to resistance. The definitions discussed earlier may have come across as focusing mostly on positive effects of power, even if the power to 'make' torture devices or 'receive' a blow to the head show that this is not in fact so. The attention to resistance in Weber's definition of power nonetheless indicates some focus on negative effects of power.

This focus on negative effects shows up more strongly in the 'intuitive idea of power' provided by Dahl in his classical article 'The Concept of Power' (1957, pp. 202–203):

> My intuitive idea of power, then, is something like this: *A* has power over *B* to the extent that he can get *B* to do something that *B* would not otherwise do.

In this definition, the relational context of power is retained, but the effect of power gets a negative connotation mostly because of the use of the word 'over'.

This attention to negative connotations of power was heightened by authors who felt that Dahl did not go far enough. In their article 'Two Faces of Power', Bachrach and Baratz argued that Dahl neglected the importance of organizing the setting within which power is exercised. In their words, addressing power in policy making:

> to the extent that a person or group – consciously or unconsciously – creates or reinforces barriers to the public airing of policy conflicts, that person or group has power.
>
> *(Bachrach & Baratz, 1962, p. 949)*

Here, power is not directly exercised by *A* over *B*, but instead *A* creates or reinforces barriers to *B*'s actions. Bachrach and Baratz refer to this process as 'the mobilization of bias' (borrowing from Schattschneider, 1960), 'nondecision-making', or the 'second face of power'. In their view, Dahl's definition of power was only concerned with public decision-making itself – the 'first face of power'.

In his book *Power: A Radical View*, Lukes argued that this still did not go far enough. According to Lukes, power is also exercised over others when it results in the change of their 'wants' – the 'third dimension of power'. As he writes:

> *A* may exercise power over *B* by getting him to do what he does not want to do, but he also exercises power over him by influencing, shaping or determining his very wants.
>
> *(Lukes, 1974, p. 23)*

In general, Lukes views the exercise of power as something negative, as it is seen to run contrary to the interests of those over whom power is exercised:

> *A* exercises power over *B* when *A* affects *B* in a manner contrary to *B*'s interests.
>
> *(ibid., p. 27)*

Not all power theorists shared this negative view of power. Around the same time at which Dahl, Bachrach and Baratz, and Lukes published their ideas, other authors emphasized positive connotations. In his article 'On the Concept of Political Power', Parsons defined power as follows:

> Power then is generalized capacity to secure the performance of binding obligations by units in a system of collective organization when the obligations are legitimized with reference to their bearing on collective goals and where in case of recalcitrance there is a presumption of enforcement by negative situational sanctions.
>
> *(Parsons, 1963, p. 308)*

Power here is seen as a capacity that supports the attainment of collective goals. It is this positive support that is argued to provide its legitimacy. But defining power in terms of supporting the attainment of collective goals excludes the possibility that a kind of power can exist that may be abused in conflict with collective goals – or with individual ones for that matter. It is a one-sided view of abilities to be referred to with the word 'power'.

In *On Violence*, Arendt also defined power as an ability that contributes to legitimate collective action:

> Power corresponds to the human ability not just to act but to act in concert. Power is never the property of an individual; it belongs to a group and remains in existence only so long as the group keeps together. When we say of somebody that he is "in power" we actually refer to his being empowered by a certain number of people to act in their name. The moment the group, from which the power originated to begin with (potestas in populo, without a people or group there is no power), disappears, "his power" also vanishes.
>
> *(Arendt, 1969, p. 44)*

Here, again, power is defined as contributing to collective goals, to act in the name of the group. Abuse of power toward the group itself or its members is excluded by definition.

Contemporary notions of power

In light of the current popularity of Foucault's ideas, it seems reasonable to start the discussion of contemporary notions of power with his idea of the meaning of 'power'. According to Foucault (1976/1978, pp. 92–93):

> power must be understood in the first instance as the multiplicity of force relations immanent in the sphere in which they operate and which constitute their own organization; as the process which, through ceaseless

struggles and confrontations, transforms, strengthens, or reverses them; as the support which these force relations find in one another, thus forming a chain or a system, or on the contrary, the disjunctions and contradictions which isolate them from one another; and lastly, as the strategies in which they take effect, whose general design or institutional crystallization is embodied in the state apparatus, in the formulation of the law, in the various social hegemonies.

According to this definition, power is a multiplicity of force relations that is processual in nature and takes effect in strategies that become embodied in social hegemonies. Thus, similar to Weber, Foucault sees power as relational. The ideas of multiplicity, process, and social hegemonies can also be found in Weber (1922, 1922/1978), but Foucault makes these ideas constitutive of his definition of power. In addition, Foucault specifically defines power as force relations, and the strategies in which these force relations take effect. The way in which force relations are embodied in social hegemonies – whichever form these may take – has been referred to as the 'fourth face of power' (Digeser, 1992).

Foucault's definition brings up the question whether power should be defined as force relations. The emphasis on force replaces the focus on abilities in the definition of power. This seems somewhat counterintuitive. It is difficult to see how having power or being in power is supposed to be understood (solely) in terms of force as commonly conceptualized. The term 'force' tends to be used to refer to a particular type of *exercise* of power – as will be described in Chapter 4. It seems more intuitive to understand having or being in power in terms of abilities – when such abilities are understood to be relative and processual (Clegg, 1989). And should strategies be seen as definitional of power? Commonly, strategies are seen to either presuppose some planning or as an interpretation of particular exercises of power – as will be discussed in Chapter 5. If power is defined in terms of strategies, the scope of the definition is limited to these cases. This seems unnecessary and counterintuitive.

Instead, a return to the centrality of abilities was suggested by Morriss (1987, p. 40) in his definition of "power as the ability to effect something". Not coincidentally, this definition is very close to that provided by Locke back in 1690. In fact, Morriss argued for the importance of 'passive power', a term he borrowed directly from Locke who used it as a synonym for the ability to receive (Morriss, ibid., p. 99; Locke, 1690/1999).

But not everyone was convinced by Morriss' suggestion. Instead, a debate ensued primarily focused on which of two terms should get precedence in understanding the meaning of power: 'power over' or 'power to'. Göhler (2009) traced the distinction between these terms to Pitkin's *Wittgenstein and Justice* (1972, p. 277), which read:

One may have *power over* another or others, and that sort of power is indeed relational…But he may have *power to* do or accomplish something all by himself, and that power is not relational at all; it may involve other people if what he has power to do is a social or political action, but it need not.

Here, 'power over' is seen as relational, whereas 'power to' is not – but this does not seem quite right. If doing something by oneself does not directly involve others, the power one needs is still relational to the natural and social context. Having the power to chop wood with an axe requires the relational ability with regard to gravity to lift the axe and it requires the relational ability with regard to the hardness of the wood to chop through it. It also requires a social situation that allows for the chopping of the wood, such as non-interference by others. Power is always relational.

This idea that power is always relational was voiced by Pansardi who proposed to use the term 'social power' instead:

> Power to and power over are best understood as two different aspects of a single, unified concept of power, which is intrinsically social and, as a consequence, able to account for the (implicit or explicit) relationality which every attribution of power involves when we talk about power in a society. Power, in a society, is always both a power over and a power to…Power to and power over…should be seen and understood as two different faces of a single concept of social power.
>
> *(Pansardi, 2012, p. 87)*

This may be so, but as power is always relational, adding the term 'social' to 'power' does not add new meaning.

Building on Arendt's definition of power, Allen (1998) argued for the importance of 'power with' in addition to 'power over' and 'power to'. The term 'power with' points to the importance of collective ability. This is certainly of great importance, but it is captured by the definition of power in terms of ability as such – as long as it is clear that ability may be collective. Collective power is discussed in Chapter 6 of this book. Kabeer (1999, p. 438) argued for the relevance of 'power within', referring to "the meaning, motivation and purpose which individuals bring to their activity, their *sense* of agency". This definition points to the importance of individual characteristics for understanding power in context. This is the subject of Chapter 3 of this book.

What arises out of this discussion is that power is a relational ability. In effect, I previously defined power in a Lockean fashion as "the relative ability to affect or receive" (Bosch, 2016, p. 35). But considering Plato's writing about the 'power to affect', which makes perfect intuitive sense, it appears superfluous to define power in combination with potential effects. Rather, power seems to be a relative ability of some kind, where the kind of ability – to effect, to affect, to make, to receive, to influence, to feel, to shape behaviors or wills of others, to work with others, to motivate oneself, to constitute social hegemonies, and so on – depends on the situation. It is this notion of power as relative ability, which is situational as well as processual, that underlies this book.

Understanding power allows for empowerment

Why is this discussion of the meaning of the word 'power' important? For one, having a clear, intuitive, notion of what the word 'power' means hampers abuse of the term. As was described in this chapter, power has sometimes been defined in rather specific ways that might be seen to support certain ideological positions. For instance, power has been defined as contributing to collective goals, but this is not always so. Or it has been defined as running against the 'interests' of those 'over' whom it is exercised, which is also not always so. Defining power in such one-sided ways leads to a distorted view of what the phenomenon is about. And such a distortion of meaning allows for an abuse of the term to promote certain perspectives rather than provide clarity. Clarifying the meaning of the word 'power' limits the possibilities for such abuse. Second, having a clear notion of the word 'power' empowers those who have it to better understand the workings of power in daily life. This may enhance abilities, both individual and collective. It creates awareness and allows for a clearer recognition of possibilities and limitations.

References

Allen, A. (1998). Power trouble: Performativity as critical theory. *Constellations*, *5*(4), 456–471. https://doi.org/10.1111/1467-8675.00108.

Arendt, H. (1969). *On violence*. New York: Harcourt, Brace and World.

Bachrach, P. & Baratz, M.S. (1962). Two faces of power. *American Political Science Review*, *56*(4), 947–952. https://doi.org/10.2307/1952796.

Bosch, R. (2016). *Power: A conceptual analysis*. The Hague: Eleven International Publishing.

Clegg, S.R. (1989). *Frameworks of power*. London: SAGE.

Dahl, R.A. (1957). The concept of power. *Behavioural Science*, *2*(3), 201–215. https://doi.org/10.1002/bs.3830020303.

Digeser, P. (1992). The fourth face of power. *The Journal of Politics*, *54*(4), 977–1007. https://doi.org/10.2307/2132105.

Foucault, M. (1976/1978). *The history of sexuality, Vol. 1: An introduction* (R. Hurley, Trans.). New York: Vintage.

Göhler, G. (2009). 'Power to' and 'power over'. In S.R. Clegg & M. Haugaard (Eds.), *The SAGE handbook of power* (pp. 27–39). London: SAGE.

Hobbes, T. (1651/1996). *Leviathan*. Oxford: Oxford University Press.

Kabeer, N. (1999). *The conditions and consequences of choice: Reflections on the measurement of women's empowerment* (Discussion Paper No. 108). United Nations Research Institute for Social Development. Retrieved 18 July 2021, from https://www.unrisd.org/80256b3c005bccf9/(httpauxpages)/31eef181bec398a380256b67005b720a/$file/dp108.pdf.

Locke, J. (1690/1999). *An essay concerning human understanding*. Hazleton: The Pennsylvania State University.

Lukes, S. (1974). *Power: A radical view*. London: Macmillan.

Morriss, P. (1987). *Power: A philosophical analysis*. Manchester: Manchester University Press.

Pansardi, P. (2012). Power to and power over: Two distinct concepts of power? *Journal of Political Power, 5*(1), 73–89. https://doi.org/10.1080/2158379X.2012.658278.

Parsons, T. (1963). On the concept of political power. *Political Studies Review, 4*(2), 124–135.

Pitkin, H.F. (1972). *Wittgenstein and justice: On the significance of Ludwig Wittgenstein for social and political thought*. Berkeley: University of California Press.

Plato (360 BC). *Sophist* (B. Jowett, Trans.). Retrieved 1 December 2020, from http://classics.mit.edu/Plato/sophist.1b.txt.

Schattschneider, E.E. (1960). *The semisovereign people: A realist's view of democracy in America*. New York: Holt, Rinehart & Winston.

Weber, M. (1922). *Gesammelte Aufsätze zur Wissenschaftslehre*. Tübingen: Verlag von J.C.B. Mohr (Paul Siebeck).

Weber, M. (1922/1978). *Economy and society* (G. Roth & C. Wittich, Eds.). Berkeley, CA: University of California Press.

2
STRUCTURES OF POWER

Relative abilities are not distributed equally. Some have more power in particular situations and areas than others, whereas others have more power in other situations and areas. The way in which relative abilities are distributed determining positions of power can be referred to as structures of power. More specifically, the term structure of power may be used to refer to an ordering of relations in terms of criteria of power. Such relations are constantly changing, as social life is a continuous process.

Structures of power are supported by sources of power, which, as will be described in this chapter, have been used to develop typologies. Actual structures of power can be analyzed using such typologies but tend not to fully conform to them; in practice, they may include elements of different typologies at the same time. Structures of power may also have particular configurations, which constitute elements of organizations that include or encompass them. Such configurations of structures of power will be discussed in Chapter 6, which is concerned with collective power. Knowledge of sources of power and typologies of structures of power empowers those that have it by providing understanding of what may be the basis for existing structures of power, and how this may affect social life. As demonstrated by Mann (2013), the typologies can be used to analyze large-scale historical developments. Knowledge of sources of power and typologies of structures of power also points to sources of power that may be used to enhance power in particular situations and areas.

Sources of power

An important criterion that has been used to distinguish structures of power is the nature of the sources of power that support them, including natural, material,

DOI: 10.4324/9781003034100-3

personal, and social ones. Hobbes' (1651/1996) definition of power presented in the previous chapter provides a first indication of what such sources may be. Faculties of body or mind can be seen as personal sources of power, certain instruments of war as material ones, and riches, reputation, friends, servants, success, and the sciences as social ones.

Natural sources of power are those sources of power that exist in nature. These can be natural resources such as water, land, oil, gas, iron, and the like, foodstuffs of various kinds, animals, plants or plant produce, climate, geographic location, air conditions, and so on. Processed natural resources may be referred to as material sources of power. These include such things as weaponry, vehicles, machines of various kinds, tools, buildings, roads, airplanes, computers, robots, and other types of products. Personal sources of power include such factors as physical strength, knowledge, and intelligence, practical and social skills, personality traits, and sense of purpose. Social sources of power include social positions, authority, norms, networks of various kinds, kinship relations, friendships, and so on, but also memberships of organizations, administrative units, social categories, and access to knowledge or the determination of it.

While these distinctions seem straightforward, in practice it is not that easy to clearly distinguish the various natural, material, personal, and social sources of power from each other. When is something that exists in nature a source of power? For this to be so, it has to be accessible and it has to be usable. Accessibility requires that some type of ownership of the natural resource is possible, and for this to be so, a system of ownership is required, which is a social source of power. In other words, natural sources of power depend on social sources of power to exist as such and are therefore, in a sense, also social sources of power. The same holds, *mutatis mutandis*, for material sources of power. Here, the relational nature of power shows up. Individual sources of power are dependent on the social context as well. Physical strength is not always a source of power, and neither are other potential individual sources of power.

Whichever be their precise nature, sources of power provide bases for structures of power. Importantly, structures of power imply that people are dependent on each other in one way or another (Emerson, 1962; Bosch, 2016). This is implicit in the idea that structures of power consist of relationships. People may be dependent in the sense of needing relationships to acquire resources, to have other people perform or abstain from performing particular actions, to receive gratifications, and so on. In other words, people may be dependent as a result of the sources of power that form the basis of other people's power. This has often been seen as determinative of the types of structures of power that can be distinguished.

Types of structures of power

Several types of structures of power have been distinguished on the basis of the sources of power that underlie them. The main types include economic power, political power, military power, ideological power, social power, cultural power, and technological power.

Economic power

The term economic power has been used to refer to structures of power based on the possession of natural, material, and/or financial resources or marketable skills; control over means of production, distribution, and exchange; and/or privileged market positions. Economic power structures include those referring to market power, as well as financial and managerial power (Weber, 1922/1978; Poggi, 2001; Mann, 2013; Bosch, 2016).

Market power refers to structures of power that exist on particular markets. These include monopoly– a market with a single seller of a product or service; monopsony – a market with a single buyer; oligopoly –a market with a limited number of sellers; oligopsony – a market with a limited number of buyers; and monopolistic competition – a market with products that are differentiated per seller. On markets, countervailing power may develop when the power of market participants leads other participants to develop market power of their own. This can include the development of regulatory agencies, consumer groups, labor unions, and buyer groups in response to the market power of sellers. Market power allows those that have it to determine prices, output levels, and market conditions (Galbraith, 1952; Olsen, 1970; Bosch, 2016).

Financial power refers to structures of power resulting from the possession or control of financial resources. Financiers provide financial resources to those who need or want them, in exchange for interest, dividends, products, positions on governing bodies, changes in organizational structures, the implementation of particular policies, or the performance of desired actions. Such a provision of financial resources can occur directly or through intervening financial markets (Albert, 1991/1993; Bosch, 2008).

Managerial power, to the extent that it is economic, is based on the ownership of means of production. When means of production are owned, employment can be offered to those who seek it, in exchange for which certain behaviors may be demanded and policies may be implemented. The extent of this type of managerial power depends on the availability of more or less skilled employees on labor markets. Managerial power may be supported by employer organizations; countervailing power may exist in the forms of labor unions or other forms of employee representation. Managerial power allows for the determination of the use of the means of production and production levels (Poggi, 2001; Bosch, 2016).

Political power

The term political power has sometimes been used to refer solely to the power of states (Mann, 2013, p. 2), but as a term such as organizational politics indicates, it can also be understood more broadly. A broad definition of politics was provided by Weber (1919/2004, p. 32), who suggested that it include "every kind of independent *leadership* activity". Importantly here, '*leadership* activity' is the translation of the German phrase '*leitender* Tätigkeit', and the meaning of the German verb '*leiten*' comes close to that of 'management'. In other words, Weber appears to use the term politics to refer to management activities, in general – including leadership. If this broad conceptualization is used, political power can be defined as managerial power – whether this refers to the management of the state or any other organization or collectivity.

Political power thus defined can be based on ownership of means of production, where it overlaps with economic power, but it can also be based on other sources of power. A source of power that has sometimes been seen as definitive of political power is the possibility to use force or sanctions. In Poggi's (2001, p. 30) words:

> What qualifies the power in question as *political* is the fact that it rests ultimately upon, and intrinsically (though often not expressly) refers to, the superior's ability to sanction coercively the subordinate's failure to comply with commands.

Another source of political power that has been distinguished is authority. Authority refers to a situation in which structures of power are considered legitimate, which means that they are perceived as desirable, proper, or appropriate (Suchman, 1995). Weber (1922/1978, p. 215) distinguished three types of authority: rational-legal, traditional, and charismatic authority, where rational-legal authority rests on "a belief in the legality of enacted rules and the right of those elevated to authority under such rules to issue commands", traditional authority on "an established belief in the sanctity of immemorial traditions and the legitimacy of those exercising authority under them", and charismatic authority on "devotion to the exceptional sanctity, heroism or exemplary character of an individual person, and of the normative patterns or order revealed or ordained by them". According to Weber, these types of authority provide the basis for corresponding types of domination (*Herrschaft*), a term he defined as "the probability that a command with a given specific content will be obeyed by a given group of people" (ibid., p. 53). This type of domination by virtue of authority is to be distinguished from domination by virtue of a constellation of interests – a term Weber used to refer to economic power based on voluntary exchange (ibid., p. 943).

In another classical analysis, Weber (1922/1978) argued that political power based on rational-legal authority is expressed most purely in the form of bureaucracy – with its formal rule-based distribution of power connected impersonally to offices rather than people, clear hierarchy, impersonal, rule-based actions, separation of staff from ownership, elaborate documentation, career paths, and selection of staff members based on technical qualifications. Where political power is based purely on traditional authority, the distribution of power is seen to depend on tradition, relations are personal, actions may be arbitrary, and recruitment occurs based on personal loyalty. This is exemplified by power structures such as patrimonialism and feudalism. If political power is based on charismatic authority, actions are thought to be based on the personal judgments of the charismatic leader – including the selection of staff members (Bosch, 2016; Clegg et al., 2019).

Other types of authority and domination have been distinguished. Willer (1967) posited the existence of ideological authority, which he saw as resting "upon *a faith in the absolute value of a rationalized set of norms*" (p. 134, emphasis in the original). Scott (1994) proposed the existence of competent domination resting on the possession of specialized knowledge or expertise. And Lukes (1995, p. 30) suggested the existence of domination that is recognition based, referring to "relations of power that result from the ability of social agents to include and exclude others from valued circles of recognition that define individuals' identities in their own eyes and in the eyes of others".

Structures of political power come in various forms. In an autocracy, political power is centralized and held by a single individual; in an oligarchy, it is held by a small group of people. Autocracies and oligarchies that are oppressive are referred to as authoritarian or totalitarian, with oppressive autocracies also referred to as tyrannies or dictatorships. Autocracies and oligarchies are examples of structures of political power in which power is held by elites. According to elitist theorists, this is inevitable (Mosca, 1939; Mills, 1956; Michels, 1962). In contrast, in a democratic structure, political power is subject to regular, free, and fair voting in contested elections. Such a structure may be more or less supported by the existence of various voluntary political collectives such as parties or platforms, diverse sources of information and communication, limitations to tenures of offices, and forms of collective decision-making. In a situation of anarchy, no person, group, or organization holds political power (Haugaard & Clegg, 2009; Tilly, 2009; Lieshout, 2011; Landemore, 2013; Bosch, 2016). According to pluralist theorists, political power in democratic countries is distributed among various interest groups in different spheres of society, depending on the particular policy fields and issues at stake. A separation of power exists between executive, legislative, and judicial powers, and political power is dispersed among governmental bodies constitutionally as well as regionally, on the basis of decision-making areas, and as a result of the existence of freedom of organization, religion, press, and education. While coalitions may form between various interests groups, these are thought to vary in permanence and not to form an oligarchy that dominates society (Polsby, 1960; Olsen, 1970).

A different way of looking at political power was suggested by Foucault. According to Foucault, the essence of structures of power lies in the 'conduct of conducts' referred to as 'government', or, in a historical context, 'governmentality' (1978/1991, p. 102, 2001, p. 341). Such government is seen to encompass "the set of institutions and practices, from administration to education, through which people's conduct is guided" (2001, p. 295). It includes 'biopower', which, on the one hand, consists of a combination of interventions and regulatory controls of biological processes such as propagation, births, health, and mortality, and on the other hand of 'disciplinary power' – constant, detailed, codified, coercive and/or gratifying (self-)surveillance of activities. According to Foucault, government has led to the development of complexes of knowledge and 'technologies of power' (ways of exercising power) that support it. The effects of government are posited to include the normalization of behavior as well as self-socialization (Foucault, 1976/1978, 1978/1991; Lemke, 2012; Clegg, 2019).

Military power

Sometimes seen as a dimension or part of political power (Poggi, 2001), military power is based on weaponry and the personal and social sources of power required to control and use it. In light of its potential expression in the form of force or violence, Mann (2013, p. 2) defined it as "the social organization of concentrated and lethal violence". Military power is usually strongly hierarchically organized and centralized, and the nature of its organization and activities requires a certain insulation from the rest of society. This tends to entail the existence of military elites. Military power may have various purposes, reaching from defending or expanding a state's territory to executing military interventions or breaking up other states. When multiple military groups exist in the territory of a single state, aims may include the destruction of other military groups, the overthrow of government, or the breaking up of the state. Military power may or may not be taken to include the power of the police and the secret service (Poggi, 2001; Mann, 2013; Ulrich, 2012).

Ideological power

Ideological power is the ability to influence the ideas, values, and norms of others on the basis of a relatively coherent set of beliefs, attitudes, and opinions (Clegg et al., 2019). It has been argued to derive from

> the human need to find ultimate meaning in life, to share norms and values, and to participate in aesthetic and ritual practices with others.
>
> *(Mann, 2013, p. 1)*

The extent of ideological power depends on status in ideological movements or communities, a status that is sometimes seen as a sacred form of authority. Ideological communities can be religious, political, or intellectual. Ideological power can be exercised in the form of the provision of religious, political, or intellectual ideas, prescriptions, gratifications, and punishments that followers accept as guiding principles (Gramsci, 1971; Foucault, 1975/1977; Mann, 1986; Poggi, 2001; Bosch, 2016).

Social power

The term 'social power' has been used in various ways. In a limited sense, it has been seen as concerned with such issues as prestige, influence, competence, knowledge, force, or authority (Bierstedt, 1950). It has also been defined as referring to control over the means of status attribution as grounded in memberships and roles of collectivities (Jessop, 1969). More generally, the term has been used to refer to distributions of power among classes, status groups, occupations, labor market participants, political parties, ethnic groups, races, genders, age groups, and other social groups. Such distributions may imply a stratification of groups with different political, social, and/or economic status (Lukes, 1995; Bosch, 2016). The term social power has also occasionally been used to refer to the power of languages and dialects (Engelstad, 2009). In the broadest sense, as discussed in the previous chapter, social power has been equated to power itself (Pansardi, 2012). The latter idea is implicit in Mann's (1986) use of the term as referring to any kind of economic, political, military, or ideological network of power. If social power is taken to refer to power based on such networks, the ability to create networks of trust that enable groups to work together toward common goals – what Boulding (1989) called 'integrative power'– may also be seen as a form of social power (Nye, 2011; Bosch, 2016).

Cultural power

Cultural power has been defined as control over the means of human value creation, interpretation, and maintenance (Jessop, 1969). In a more general sense, it may be seen as referring to the relative ability to affect or be affected by structures of meaning (Geertz, 1973; Swidler, 1995). It encompasses what Goldman (1972, p. 263) referred to as the power to persuade – the power with regard to psychological states of others, such as desires, beliefs, and attitudes. It may also be seen to include what Castells (2009) called 'communication power' – the power embedded in the mass media and communication networks to affect culture by symbolic means. Cultural power has also been taken to refer to the power to affect the meaning embedded in social practices and institutions (Bourdieu, 1972/1977; Foucault, 1976/1978; Swidler, 1995).

Technological power

Technological power is based on technologies, which will here be taken to refer to practices of designing and creating artifacts and artificial processes and systems. Such practices include the production of goods and artifact-based services, the building of tools, machines, and infrastructures of various kinds, as well as processes of mechanization and automation, cybernetic systems, and software development. Technologies in their turn are based on various types of knowledge, including specific scientific, design, production, and operational knowledge as well as knowledge embedded in data and networks (Mumford, 1934, 1964; Feenberg, 2017; Franssen et al., 2018; Harari, 2019).

Technologies may support or undermine structures of power by means of their application, but they may also embody particular structures of power as a result of what is required for their functioning. Certain technologies may be effective under centralistic and top-down decision-making, whereas other technologies may be effective when decision-making is dispersed and bottom-up. Technologies can also have more or less intended side effects that support or undermine particular structures of power, for instance, resulting from implemented design features or the way in which technologies are used in practice (Mumford, 1964; Winner, 1980; Sclove, 1992; Feenberg, 2017).

Characteristics of structures of power

Although the various types of power can be conceptually separated, in real life they exist in mixed and intermingled forms. Different types of power may coincide with, support, or undermine other types and vice versa. Thus, economic power depends on political organization, regulation, and enforcement, while political power requires economic power to support it with economic resources. Ideological power supports political power by imbuing those subject to it with ideas, values, and norms which provide legitimacy. Reversely, political power supports ideological power by providing the organization, regulation, and enforcement it needs. Economic power also requires legitimacy that may be provided in the form of ideas, values, and norms supporting it, while economic power provides economic resources supporting ideological power. Social, cultural, and technological power also require economic power to provide economic resources, while economic power depends on social networks, the provision of meaning by cultural power, and the effectiveness of technologies. Social, cultural, and technological power depend on political support as well as ideological legitimation, and, in their turn, political power and ideological power are dependent on social cultural, and technological power (Poggi, 2001; Castells, 2009; Bosch, 2016; Feenberg, 2017).

The particular mix of different types of power may have various configurations. For any such configuration, a distinction can be made between superior positions of domination, as defined earlier, and inferior positions of subordination. When domination exists over a large part of society, it is referred to as hegemony (Gramsci, 1971; Dowding, 2012). Many configurations of structures of power exist in the shape of formal and informal organizational structures and their characteristics. Such configurations are discussed in Chapter 6, which deals with collective power.

While always changing to some extent, structures of power may be relatively stable or, alternatively, experience significant change. A relative stability of structures of power may result when they are taken for granted as normal, natural, or rational. Different types and configurations of structures of power can support each other in such a way that it becomes difficult to conceive of any significant structural change. Structures of power are also supported by those aspiring to become part of them or take advantage of them (Weber, 1922/1978; Powell & DiMaggio, 1991). Resistance to structures of power may exist based on alternative structures of power. More specifically, resistance consists of alternative exercises of power dependent on underlying structures of power. Where resistance is met with exercises of power emanating from dominating structures, conflicts may arise. Resistance and conflicts can lead to significant changes in structures of power when they effect changes in sources of power underlying the dominating structures (Olsen, 1970; Weber, 1922/1978; Scott, 2001; Bosch, 2016).

Structures of power and empowerment

Knowledge is a source of power, and sources of power underlie structures of power. In other words, to those that have it, knowledge about sources of power and types of structures of power provides power in relationships. Knowledge about types of structures of power also provides the ability to recognize, analyze, and understand structures of power. An example of this empowering effect is provided by Mann (2013), who pointed to the importance of capitalism (economic power), nation states (political power), military strike ranges (military power), and the ideologies of liberalism and socialism (ideological power) for understanding globalization and its development.

References

Albert, M. (1991/1993). *Capitalism against capitalism* (P. Haviland, Trans.). London: Whurr Publishers.

Bierstedt, R. (1950). An analysis of social power. *American Sociological Review, 15,* 730–738. https://doi.org/10.2307/2086605.

Bosch, R. (2008). *Bringing nuance into the globalization debate: Changes in US, Japanese, and German management, with special reference to the impact of international finance,* EUI PhD theses. Retrieved 1 December 2020, from http://cadmus.eui.eu/handle/1814/9987.

Bosch, R. (2016). *Power: A conceptual analysis.* The Hague: Eleven International Publishing.

Boulding, K.E. (1989). *Three faces of power.* Newbury Park, CA: SAGE.

Bourdieu, P. (1972/1977). *Outline of a theory of practice* (R. Nice, Trans.). Cambridge: Cambridge University Press.

Castells, M. (2009). *Communication power.* Oxford: Oxford University Press.

Clegg, S. (2019). Governmentality. *Project Management Journal, 50*(3), 266–270. https://doi.org/10.1177/8756972819841260.

Clegg, S., Kornberger, M., Pitsis, T.S., & Mount, M. (2019). *Managing & organizations: An introduction to theory and practice* (5th ed.). Los Angeles, CA: SAGE.

Dowding, K. (2012). Why should we care about the definition of power? *Journal of Political Power, 5*(1), 119–135. https://doi.org/10.1080/2158379X.2012.661917.

Emerson, R.M. (1962). Power-dependence relations. *American Sociological Review, 27,* 31–41. https://doi.org/10.2307/2089716.

Engelstad, F. (2009). Culture and power. In S.R. Clegg & M. Haugaard (Eds.), *The SAGE handbook of power* (pp. 210–238). Thousand Oaks, CA: SAGE.

Feenberg, A. (2017). *Technosystem: The social life of reason.* Cambridge, MA: Harvard University Press.

Foucault, M. (1975/1977). *Discipline and punish: The birth of the prison* (A. Sheridan, Trans.). New York: Random House.

Foucault, M. (1976/1978). *The history of sexuality, vol. 1: An introduction* (R. Hurley, Trans.). New York: Vintage.

Foucault, M. (1978/1991). Governmentality. In G. Burchell, C. Gordon, & P. Miller (Eds.), *The Foucault Effect: Studies in governmentality* (pp. 87–104). Chicago, IL: The University of Chicago Press.

Foucault, M. (2001). *Power* (J.D. Faubion, Ed.; R. Hurley & others, Trans.). New York: The New Press.

Franssen, M., Lokhorst, G.-J., & Van de Poel, I. (2018). Philosophy of technology. *Stanford Encyclopedia of Philosophy.* Retrieved 5 January 2021, from https://plato.stanford.edu/entries/technology/.

Galbraith, J.K. (1952). *American capitalism.* Boston, MA: Houghton Mifflin.

Geertz, C. (1973). *The interpretation of cultures: Selected essays by Clifford Geertz.* New York: Basic Books.

Goldman, A.I. (1972). Towards a theory of social power. *Philosophical Studies, 23*(4), 221–268. https://doi.org/10.1007/BF00356228.

Gramsci, A. (1971). *Selections from the prison notebooks* (Q. Hoare & G.N. Smith, Trans.). New York: International Publishers.

Harari, Y.N. (2019). *21 Lessons for the 21st Century.* London: Vintage.

Haugaard, M. & Clegg, S.R. (2009). Introduction: Why power is the central concept of the social sciences. In S.R. Clegg & M. Haugaard (Eds.), *The SAGE handbook of power* (pp. 1–24). Thousand Oaks, CA: SAGE.

Hobbes, T. (1651/1996). *Leviathan.* Oxford: Oxford University Press.

Jessop, R.D. (1969). Exchange and power in structural analysis. *Sociological Review, 17,* 415–431. https://doi.org/10.1111/j.1467-954X.1969.tb01194.x.

Landemore, H. (2013). *Democratic reason: Politics, collective intelligence, and the rule of the many.* Princeton, NJ: Princeton University Press.

Lemke, T. (2012). *Foucault, governmentality, and critique.* London: Routledge.

Lieshout, R.H. (2011). Anarchy in international relations. In K. Dowding (Ed.), *Encyclopedia of Power* (pp. 20–22). Los Angeles, CA: SAGE.

Lukes, S. (1995). Power. Paper presented at the European University Institute, Florence, Italy.

Mann, M. (1986). *The sources of social power. Vol. 1: A history of power from the beginning to A.D. 1760.* Cambridge: Cambridge University Press.

Mann, M. (2013). *The sources of social power. Vol. 4: Globalizations, 1945–2011.* Cambridge: Cambridge University Press.

Michels, R. (1962). *Political parties* (E. Paul & C. Paul, Trans.). New York: The Free Press.

Mills, C.W. (1956). *The power elite.* New York: Oxford University Press.

Mosca, G. (1939). *The ruling class* (A. Livingstone, Ed. & Trans.). New York: McGraw-Hill.

Mumford, L. (1934). *Technics and civilization.* London: Routledge & Kegan Paul.

Mumford, L. (1964). Authoritarian and democratic technics. *Technology and Culture, 5*(1), 1–8. https://doi.org/10.2307/3101118.

Nye, J.S. (2011). Power and foreign policy. *Journal of Political Power, 4*(1), 9–24. https://doi.org/10.1080/2158379X.2011.555960.

Olsen, M.E. (1970). *Power in societies.* New York: Macmillan.

Pansardi, P. (2012). Power to and power over: Two distinct concepts of power? *Journal of Political Power, 5*(1), 73–89. https://doi.org/10.1080/2158379X.2012.658278.

Poggi, G. (2001). *Forms of power.* Cambridge: Polity.

Polsby, N.W. (1960). How to study community power: The pluralist alternative. *Journal of Politics, 22*(3), 474–484. https://doi.org/10.2307/2126892.

Powell, W.W. & DiMaggio, P.J. (Eds.) (1991). *The new institutionalism in organizational analysis.* Chicago, IL: The University of Chicago Press.

Sclove, R.E. (1992). The nuts and bolts of democracy: Democratic theory and technological design. In L. Winner (Ed.), *Democracy in a technological society* (pp. 139–157). Dordrecht: Springer Science+Business Media.

Scott, J. (Ed.) (1994). *Power: Critical concepts.* London: Routledge.

Scott, J. (2001). *Power.* Cambridge: Polity.

Suchman, M.C. (1995). Managing legitimacy: Strategic and institutional approaches. *Academy of Management Review, 20*(3), 571–610. https://doi.org/10.5465/amr.1995.9508080331.

Swidler, A. (1995). *Cultural power and social movements.* In H. Johnston & B. Klandermans (Eds.), *Social movements, protests, and contention. Volume 4* (pp. 25–40). Minneapolis: University of Minnesota Press.

Tilly, C. (2009). Power and democracy. In S.R. Clegg & M. Haugaard (Eds.), *The SAGE handbook of power* (pp. 70–88). Thousand Oaks, CA: SAGE.

Ulrich, M.P. (2012). A primer on civil-military relations for senior leaders. In J.B. Bartholomees, Jr. (Ed.), *U.S. Army War College guide to national security issues. Volume II: National security policy and strategy* (pp. 306–316). Carlisle, PA: Strategic Studies Institute.

Weber, M. (1919/2004). Politics as a vocation. In D. Owen & T.B. Strong (Eds.), R. Livingstone (Trans.), *The vocation lectures* (pp. 32–94). Indianapolis, IN: Hackett Publishing.

Weber, M. (1922/1978). *Economy and society* (G. Roth & C. Wittich, Eds.). Berkeley: University of California Press.

Willer, D.E. (1967). Max Weber's missing authority type. *Sociological Inquiry, 37*(2): 231–239. https://doi.org/10.1111/j.1475-682X.1967.tb00652.x.

Winner, L. (1980). Do artifacts have politics? *Daedalus, 109*(1), 121–136.

3
INDIVIDUAL POWER

In this book, the term individual power will be used to refer to the power that results from the personal characteristics of an individual in context. These characteristics develop during the process that constitutes an individual's lifetime as well as through an individual's internal processes. The latter include biological, goal-oriented, emotional, cognitive, and action-oriented processes, all occurring within developmental and environmental processes (M.E. Ford, 1992; D.H. Ford, 2013). The environment, too, consists of processes, such as those occurring in families, neighborhoods, educational institutions, work places, and online. The natural, social, and technological environments continuously change.

This processual and situational perspective forms the background to this chapter on individual power. Similar to the concept of structure, concepts referring to individual power – such as goals, emotions, cognitions, personality, self, and identity – run the risk of being taken to refer to stable characteristics. But these concepts, indispensable as they are for understanding individual power, should all be seen as referring to situational and continuously changing characteristics. Such changes may vary in extent, from barely noticeable to highly significant.

A useful concept to capture the processual development of individual power as a result of the functioning of the brain is the idea of behavior episode schemata – representations of neural structures in the brain – as proposed by Ford (1987, 2013). This idea will be discussed in the following section. The importance of goals, emotions, cognitions, personality, self, and identities will be discussed next as they come together in and affect the power individuals have in their decision-making and actions within their social context. A phenomenon that has recently become prominent is what may be called 'techno-adjusted' individual power – individual power adjusted by technologies that work in the body or through interfaces that are close to the body. Technologies that work in the body primarily include those resulting from biotechnical research in genetic and

DOI: 10.4324/9781003034100-4

molecular engineering. Other important technologies derive from research and developments in ICT in the fields of networking, data science, AI, and robotics – technologies that may adjust individual power through interfaces ranging from desktops, laptops, cell phones, watches, and glasses to various types of implants. Techno-adjusted individual power will be discussed in the penultimate section of this chapter, after which consequences for empowerment will be noted.

Behavior episode schemata

The idea behind behavior episode schemata is that, while living, individuals go through so-called 'behavior episodes'. As described by Ford (2013, p. 149), a behavior episode may be represented as:

> a pattern of behavior which extends over a period of time and has the following attributes: (a) some set of consequences towards which it is directed…; (b) a variable pattern of activities… selectively organized with feed forward and feedback to try to produce those consequences; (c) a set of environmental circumstances within which and towards which the behavior is directed; and (d) a termination of the pattern when (1.) the consequences toward which the episode is directed occur, or (2.) some circumstances within or without the person change, preempting an episode because some alternate consequences have become more important, interesting, or possible at that time, or (3.) the evaluation of progress leads to the conclusion that the consequences are unobtainable – at least for the moment.

In other words, a behavior episode consists of a pattern of activities oriented at a set of consequences within certain environmental circumstances. Behavior episodes may be instrumental, emotional, observational, and/or thinking episodes.

Living through a behavior episode leads to the construction of an episodic memory. When a similar behavior episode is lived through, such an episodic memory is activated and elaborated into a mental structure – a behavior episode schema. Such a schema includes mental representations of biological, goal-oriented, emotional, cognitive, action-oriented, and environmental processes that play a role in similar behavior episodes. Different behavior episode schemata are constructed as a result of different behavior episodes that are lived through. They may become combined, revised, elaborated, reconstructed, or diluted due to similarities or differences that occur during behavior episodes that share similarities that activate existing behavior episode schemata.

The concept of behavior episode schemata shows how goal-oriented, emotional, cognitive, action-oriented, and environmental processes together lead to the development of individual mental capacities in the sense of mental structures that include representations of those processes. This starts in the womb, ends at death, and depends on and is consistent with biological and neurological processes and capabilities (Ford, 2013; Kandel et al., 2013). It is this developmental conceptualization of individual power in context which underlies the subsequent discussion of more commonly used concepts concerned with individual power.

Which goals may underlie individual power?

Individual power is influenced by the goals individuals may have in their behavior episode schemata. An individual with the strong goal to attain power may well be more powerful in interactions with others than an individual with the strong goal to avoid anxiety. Of course, this depends on the particular abilities that are under consideration and the situation in which individuals find themselves. But in order to be able to perceive, analyze, evaluate, and understand individual power, a discussion of goals is helpful.

This discussion is an ancient one. Plato (375 BC) made a distinction between the principles of reason, desire, and passion, while Aristotle (350 BCa) distinguished activities as ends in themselves from ends produced through activities. Individual goals were also discussed by philosophers and psychologists such as Descartes, Spinoza, James, Freud, McDougall, Murray, and Russell (Reiss, 2004). A popular classification of goals was presented by Maslow (1943) in the form of a hierarchy of human needs ranging from physiological needs at the bottom to self-actualization needs at the top. Ford and Nichols developed a taxonomy of human goals consisting of a list of desired within-person consequences that may be affective, cognitive, or subjective organizational, and desired person-environment consequences, including self-assertive social relationship goals, integrative social relationship goals, and task goals. In their view, whether or not a hierarchical relationship exists between different goals is an empirical question (Ford, 1992).

More recently, Reiss (2004) presented a list of 16 basic desires, which he derived by means of factor analyses of the results of a range of empirical surveys using a wide-ranging list of potential goals. The basic desires distinguished by Reiss are: power, curiosity, independence, status, social contact, vengeance, honor, idealism, physical exercise, romance, family, order, eating, acceptance, tranquility, and saving. These basic desires are to be seen as empirically separate, or, as Reiss (2004, p. 186) put it, they constitute a multi-faceted model of intrinsic motives. The relevance of these intrinsic motives may differ within and between individuals. According to Reiss, an individual will typically be striving to satisfy various motives to a certain desired extent. When a particular motive is strong, an individual will strive to satisfy that motive to a high extent. Thus, an individual with a strong power motive will strive to satisfy the desire for power. Other desires distinguished by Reiss may support or undermine individual power in various ways. For instance, curiosity may support the acquirement of knowledge which constitutes a source of power, while tranquility may limit the acquisition of sources of power. More generally, basic desires influence and are influenced by other elements of behavior episode schemata, thereby impacting on individual power.

Long-term individual goals have been referred to as 'values'. Early empirical research into individual values was performed by Rokeach (1973), who developed a value survey based on existing literature. He distinguished personal and social values on the one hand, and moral and competence values on the other. Building on Rokeach's work, while elaborating the approach taken both theoretically and empirically, Schwartz (1992) posited the world-wide existence of ten value types. In a later empirical study, Schwartz et al. (2012) distinguished 19 individual values on the basis of the analysis of data from 10 different countries using factor analysis and multidimensional scaling. The values distinguished by Schwartz et al. are self-direction-thought, self-direction-action, stimulation, hedonism, achievement, power-resources, power-dominance, face, security-personal, security-societal, tradition, conformity-rules, conformity-interpersonal, humility, benevolence-dependability, benevolence-caring, universalism-concern, universalism-nature, and universalism-tolerance.

These values may or may not conflict with each other. Schwartz et al. found that values concerned with self-protection and avoiding anxiety (conformity, tradition, security, face, and power) tended to be opposed to values that express anxiety-free growth (benevolence, universalism, self-direction, stimulation, and hedonism). Values focused on personal outcomes (self-direction, stimulation, hedonism, achievement, power, and face) were found to contradict values focused on social outcomes (tradition, humility, benevolence, and universalism). Values concerned with self-transcendence (benevolence and universalism) opposed values concerned with self-enhancement (power and achievement). And values concerned with conservation (conformity and tradition) contradicted values concerned with openness to change (self-direction and stimulation). Whereas differences exist between the list of 16 basic desires suggested by Reiss and the values distinguished by Schwartz et al., commonalities also exist. Both studies mention power, stimulation and tranquility are (inversely) related, self-direction is similar to independence, and so are universalism and idealism and tradition and honor.

What can be said about these findings of basic desires and values? Well, they provide tools that can help in interpreting individual power. It helps to know which goals and values may play a role in a particular situation to understand one's own or someone else's individual power, as these goals and values interact with existing behavior episode schemata, individual actions, and the situational context. Might someone's value be that of power or universalism? This can make a big difference in the interpretation of individual power. It is also helpful to know that values can be contradictory, and that multiple goals and values may be more or less guiding in particular behavior episodes. Knowing about goals and values empowers those that do to come up with plausible interpretations of what is going on when power is at stake.

At the same time, it is important to note that the research by Reiss and Schwartz et al. is based on cross-cultural statistical research. This type of research – which aims at cross-culturally statistically validated findings – by its nature glosses over subtle differences of meaning of goals and values and excludes those that are unique for different people and groups. This means that this type of research should be placed within an interpretive context. Are the desires and values suggested by Reiss and Schwartz useful for a particular interpretation, or is there a need for a more comprehensive cultural psychological approach which retains subtle differences in meaning and uniqueness (Ratner, 2008)? Is it better to take an anthropological approach with specific individual goals constituting categories derived from interpretation (Geertz, 1973)? Whichever the case may be, the ideas developed by Reiss and Schwartz et al. offer clarity concerning goals and values, whether such clarity is used constructively or critically. Their basic desires and universal values can be used in interpretation as sensitizing concepts—concepts that help to think about particular subjects and that may or may not be included, or with modification, in an overall interpretation (Blumer, 1954).

Emotions and power

Emotions may play important roles when power is concerned. Fear, love, compassion, hatred, contempt – these emotions figure prominently in Sun's *The Art of War* and Machiavelli's *The Prince*. Individuals' power may depend on the extent to which they experience certain emotions as well as on the extent to which others in their social environment do. But what are emotions? Here, again, the debate is an ancient one. In *Rhetoric*, Aristotle (350 BCb) wrote:

> The Emotions are all those feelings that so change men as to affect their judgements, and that are also attended by pain or pleasure.

According to Aristotle, such emotions come in several dimensions of opposites. These include anger-calmness, friendship-enmity, fear-confidence, shame-shamelessness, kindness–unkindness, pity-indignation, and emulation-contempt. To understand such emotions, Aristotle pointed to the importance of state of mind, the social environment, and the grounds that stir them. Subsequent to Aristotle, several philosophers and psychologists discussed emotions including Descartes, Darwin, James, Dewey, and Freud (Keltner et al., 2013; Scarantino, 2016).

More recently, Frijda and Mesquita (1994, p. 51) defined emotions as follows:

> Emotions... are affective responses to what happens in the environment and cognitive representations of the event's meaning for the individual. They are, first and foremost, modes of relating to the environment: states of readiness for engaging, or not engaging, in interaction with that environment.

Emotions constitute dynamic processes within social contexts. During behavior episodes, the meaning of emotions is affected by social interactions within a cultural context. What this means is that while certain basic emotions can be distinguished, the precise meaning of such emotions depends on the situation (Mesquita, 2010; Mesquita et al., 2016). Emotions can have a strong impact on how someone perceives, thinks, and acts. The immediate attention that may accompany them may overwhelm existing patterns of perception, thinking, and acting, to some extent replacing them with automated patterns (Ford, 2013; Bosch, 2016).

Izard (2011) distinguished a number of emotions that he considered 'basic': interest, joy, sadness, anger, and fear. These emotions are deemed basic because relative to other emotions, they are thought to have a simple structure, a specific function, and direct importance to survival and well-being. More complex emotions, such as jealousy and envy, are seen to be constituted by several interacting emotions and are thought to interact more extensively with goals and cognitions.

Basic or not, emotions come with particular states of readiness for engaging or not engaging. Thus, according to Ford (2013), the emotion of interest promotes exploratory and investigatory behavior in contexts that involve novelty or variability within familiar boundaries. Joy motivates people to continue behavior episodes in which they are making progress toward their goals, as well as to repeat behavior episodes in which they have successfully achieved their goals. Sadness is thought to facilitate the termination of unsuccessful behavior episodes. Fear helps people avoid or proceed cautiously in circumstances involving real or potential threats to their psychological or physical well-being. And anger is seen to produce behaviors such as aggression, protest, social activism, or highly energized activity characterized by intense determination. These (functionalist) descriptions appear plausible, but some criticism has been leveled against them. The states of readiness may be more complex, or they may be culturally dependent (Feldman Barrett et al., 2016). More specifically, the specific states of readiness connected to emotions depend on the particular elaboration of behavior episode schemata of an individual in context. Still, Ford's descriptions give plausible impressions that can be useful to an interpretation of the role of emotions in individual power.

Ford (2013) also described states of readiness for engaging or not engaging for more complex emotions. Thus, surprise is seen to interrupt behavior episodes and to reorient focal attention so that sudden, unexpected events can be evaluated for their potential personal significance. Disgust is thought to help people avoid contaminated environments. Sexual arousal facilitates the initiation and repetition of sexual encounters. Love facilitates cooperative social functioning, the development of satisfying interpersonal relationships, and the sheltering and nourishing of helpless people, by supporting the process of interpersonal bonding and the development of mutual commitment and trust. Grief is thought to help people cope with the loss of meaningful and cherished relationships by encouraging union and reunion with significant others. Shame encourages people to stay within the boundaries of group constraints such as those defined by social norms, moral values, and rules of conduct. It supports conformity, obedience, and socially responsible behavior. Jealousy is seen to facilitate the use of coercive, corrective actions against people who are disrupting or not conforming to existing or desired social arrangements. It is thought to help people protect themselves against real or imagined threats to their social values, interests, and relationships. Finally, contempt is seen to encourage people to reject others from a social group or relationship or to influence those others to behave better when they have committed a social transgression or behaved in an unacceptable, offensive, or incompetent manner (Ford, 1992, 2013; Bosch, 2016). Here again, the (functionalist) descriptions provided by Ford appear plausible, but they may be criticized for not being sufficiently complex or culturally sensitive (Feldman Barrett et al., 2016).

Other emotions have been distinguished with states of readiness for engaging or not engaging connected to them. The emotions of gratitude and compassion have been seen as helping to build social capital and well-being (DeSteno et al., 2016), and empathy as supporting vital helping, cooperative and generous behavior through prosocial motivation (Zaki & Ochsner, 2016). Many other emotions have been distinguished with potential states of readiness (Watt Smith, 2016). The importance of an understanding of emotions to the analysis of individual power consists in the potentially overwhelming and immediate effect they may have on goals, cognitions, and actions. This is why such importance was attached to them by those with a practical interest into the workings of power such as Sun and Machiavelli.

Thinking

The term 'thinking' refers to the processing of information in the brain. This process contains a number of sub-processes – attention, perception, remembering, cognition, and decision-making – that all have clear relevance to (understanding) an individual's power. Starting with the process of attention, this is concerned with the way in which the brain controls the allocation of its limited capacity for gathering information. Due to the limited capacity of the brain, by necessity only a limited number of informational items are selected as relevant while others are ignored. Informational items that are intense, readily available, under personal control, and/or most relevant to current concerns are more likely to be attended to than other informational items. Attention processes may become habitual, focusing on similar informational items in similar behavior episodes. At the same time, the development of habits in behavior episode schemata allows more room for attention to be paid to novel informational items (Ford, 1992; Styles, 2006; Kahneman, 2011; Bosch, 2016).

Processes of attention play an important role in perception. To a significant extent, the perception of informational items depends on attention being focused on them, although evidence exists that some perception may occur without significant attention (Styles, 2006; Grondin, 2016). As perceptions occur during behavior episodes, they activate existing behavior episode schemata that have similarities to such behavior episodes. These activated behavior episode schemata provide interpretations to the perceptions which may activate other behavior episode schemata. This way, perceptions may lead to elaborations or modifications of behavior episode schemata at different levels of abstraction as well as activate particular goals, emotions, and thought and/or action patterns. Interpretations of perceptions that are consistent with existing behavior episode schemata are thought to be accommodated relatively easily, whereas interpretations of perceptions that contrast with existing behavior episode schemata may be rejected or, alternatively, lead to a rearrangement of behavior episode schemata (Ford, 1992, 2013; March & Simon, 1993; Kahneman, 2011; Bosch, 2016).

The elaboration of behavior episode schemata includes the construction of memory. Different types of memory have been distinguished: sensory, short-term/working, and long-term memory. Interpretations of sensory information stored in short-term/working memory may become part of long-term memory if they fit well with existing long-term behavior episode schemata, are repeated, important, and/or supported by goals and/or emotions, or if cognitive techniques such as mnemonics and retrieval are used. In their turn, both long-term and short-term/working memory affect processes of attention that influence the construction of sensory memory. Such invocations of memory lead to reconstructions of past experiences, abstract levels of knowledge, and personal meanings that may differ from behavior episode to behavior episode. Memories may become strengthened, modified, or they may fade (Kahneman, 2011; Ford, 2013; Baddeley et al., 2014; Halpern, 2014; Bosch, 2016; McCrudden & McNamara, 2017).

Behavior episode schemata also constitute thought patterns, which may be referred to as cognitions. Behavior episode schemata at various levels of abstraction may be combined to constitute thinking episodes. During a thinking episode, behavior episode schemata containing goals, perceptions, emotions, memories, and cognitions are activated and merged in various ways until a level of satisfaction has been reached that ends the thinking episode (March & Simon, 1993; Gilovich & Griffin, 2010; Kahneman, 2011; Ford, 2013; Bosch, 2016). Because thinking is an effortful activity, often only a limited number of merges of behavior episode schemata are attempted. What results is what Simon (1979) referred to as 'bounded rationality', a process in which – due to limitations of mental capacities – the search for information is selective and the outcome of thinking aims at satisfaction rather than optimization.

In 'exploring the territory of bounded rationality', Kahneman (2003, 2011) came to distinguish two main systems of thinking. In 'System 1', thinking is fast, automatic, effortless, associative, implicit, habitual, and often emotionally charged. Thinking in 'System 2' is slow, serial, effortful, flexible, rule-governed, and often monitored and deliberately controlled. Thought processes belonging to System 1 can easily be combined with other thought processes, whereas System 2 thought processes tend to interfere with each other.

In System 1 thought processes, important roles are played by so-called 'heuristics'– habitual short-cuts in thinking processes aimed at finding acceptable solutions relatively fast. The use of such heuristics may be effective, but heuristics may also be applied incorrectly. Kahneman (2011) described the following heuristics:

- priming (giving stronger weight to initial than subsequent information)
- confirmation bias (seeking information that is consistent with existing ideas)
- the halo effect (the tendency to like or dislike everything about a person)
- intensity matching (matching evaluations across different dimensions)
- the law of small numbers (using a small sample)
- anchoring (adjusting a base value)
- availability (using readily available information)
- representativeness (using similarity, including unsubstantiated extrapolation and the use of stereotypes)
- selecting a plausible description over a more probable one
- giving more weight to causal stories than to statistics
- attributing cause when there is luck or coincidence and vice versa
- hindsight bias (underestimating the extent to which past events were surprising)
- outcome bias (focusing on outcomes instead of the process that led to it)
- loss aversion (being more averse to losses than foregone gains)
- an unsubstantiated belief in correlation between variables
- the inability to apply a given set of criteria consistently

Based on his research of marketing practices, Cialdini (2009) added the following heuristics to the list:

- reciprocation (being led by a sense of obligation to reciprocate)
- commitment and consistency (being consistent with previous commitments)
- social proof (looking at others for correct behavior)
- liking (being guided by liking and disliking)
- authority (being guided by obedience to authority)
- scarcity (attaching more value to scarce opportunities than to others)

Other heuristics include (Zimbardo & Leippe, 1991; Vohs & Luce, 2010):

- recency (giving strong weight to information that is provided most recently)
- psychological reactance (a tendency to reassert freedom by non-conformity)
- attraction (when two options are closely matched, choosing the one that compares favorably to a newly introduced option)
- compromise (when faced with options that trade off one feature for another, choosing the one in the middle)
- the tendency to diversify

The slow, deliberate, and effortful form of thinking of System 2 may include the use of various types of logic up to and including Aristotelian deduction, induction, and abduction (Peirce, 1896/1931; Bosch, 2012). When it is ori-ented at reaching decisions, a number of phases may be distinguished. The first phase has been called 'identification'. During this phase, the need to make particular decisions is recognized, and ideas are formed about the types of decisions to be made. In one form or another, this includes a formulation of problems to be solved. In the 'generation' stage, options for decisions come to the fore. In this stage of problem solving and plan formulation, alternative solutions and plans are constructed based on relevant behavior episodes and behavior episode schemata. This includes processes of information gathering, processing, and remembering as well as emotional and cognitive processes. A third stage that has been distinguished is that of 'judgment' or evaluation, during which different solutions and plans are evaluated. These three processes can be seen as intermingled and iterative (March & Simon, 1993; Ford, 2013; Minda, 2015).

During decision-making, options that are under immediate personal control tend to be considered first. This way, habitual ways of deciding may lead to the rejection of novel ideas and information. If this does not lead to a satisfying solution, other options may be considered and information about these options may be gathered. If this still does not lead to a satisfactory course of action, evaluative criteria may be relaxed. During this process, emotional processes can make certain options unavailable or desirable, and so can the costs and benefits connected to particular decisions. Overall, a decision-making process may be well-structured and logical, but it may also be messy and ad hoc with lapses in logical thinking and interference of various heuristics and emotions (Etzioni, 1991; March & Simon, 1993; Vohs & Luce, 2010; Ford, 2013; Minda, 2015; Bosch, 2016).

Understanding the thinking process empowers by means of the insights it offers into one's own and other people's thinking capabilities and particularities. It also provides access points for exercises of power over others or by others – as will become clear in the next chapter.

Personality

Similar to the other concepts discussed in this chapter, the study of personality has a long history. In *Nicomachean Ethics*, Aristotle (350BCa) distinguished 12 virtuous characteristics of individuals: courage, temperance in the sphere of pleasure and pain, liberality and magnificence in getting and spending, am-bition and magnanimity in honor, patience, truthfulness, wittiness, friendli-ness, modesty, and righteous indignation. This focus on moral character traits can be found in subsequent works of philosophers such as Hume, Marx, Mill, and Rawls (Homiak, 2019). In psychology, the field of personality research became established in the 1930s as a result of the works of Allport and Murray (Larsen & Buss, 2017).

Larsen and Buss (2017, p. 4, emphasis in the original) provide the following definition of personality:

> **Personality** is the set of psychological traits and mechanisms within the individual that are organized and relatively enduring and that influence his or her interactions with, and adaptations to, the intrapsychic, physical, and social environments.

Traits and mechanisms refer to individual differences and similarities between people that are reflected in their goals, emotions, thoughts, and behaviors (Carver, 2010; Larsen & Buss, 2017). Contemporary psychological research has tended to make a distinction between five main personality traits in a thoroughly tested taxonomy known as the five-factor model. These personality traits are (Funder & Fast, 2010):

- extraversion: the degree to which an individual is outgoing, energetic, and experiences positive emotion
- neuroticism: the degree to which an individual worries, is reactive to stress and experiences negative emotion
- conscientiousness: the degree to which an individual is dependable, organized, and punctual
- agreeableness: the degree to which an individual is cooperative, warm, and gets along well with others
- openness to experience: the degree to which an individual is creative, open-minded, and aesthetic

On the basis of empirical research, it has been proposed that extraverted people interact well with strangers, and are committed to their work where they often assume leadership positions. People who are neurotic are thought to have difficulties in interactions, relationships, and job performance. Conscientious people have been seen work hard, to be punctual, perfectionist, persevering, and reliable, and to be satisfied with their jobs and relationships. Agreeable individuals have been found to be empathic, prosocial, and likeable, and to avoid social conflict while preferring harmonious and cooperative interactions. Those individuals that are open to experience are thought to like new experiences, and to be creative and unprejudiced (John et al., 2008; Carver, 2010; Bosch, 2016; Larsen & Buss, 2017).

The five-factor model may exclude other personality traits that have been suggested; it may also exclude culturally dependent personality traits. Moreover, personality traits should not be considered as stable as changes in personality may occur (Larsen & Buss, 2017). The theories based on the five-factor model have an ideal typical character, meaning that it is unlikely to find actual cases that are fully described by them. As with other ideas discussed in this chapter, the five-factor model and theories based on it may nonetheless be useful for the interpretation of individual power.

The self and identities

In an Aristotelian sense, 'the self' can be seen to refer to an existing awareness of an embodied psyche through which an individual relates to the world (Aristotle, 350 BC; Sorabji, 2008). This overarching self can be differentiated into various identities – sets of meanings that define who one is on the basis of one's characteristics, roles, or memberships (Burke & Stets, 2009).

The meanings that are seen as definitional for a person's identities may arise from existing perceptions, goals, emotions, memories, and cognitions, and reactions from and comparisons with people in the social environment. The particular identities that are salient in specific times and places depend upon cues that activate them. Identities at home often differ from identities at work and from those at social events. Identities also depend on existing and salient social categories, such as those of gender, race, class, nationality, and various groups and communities. Status hierarchies, worldviews, and elements of culture also influence identities. The identities that are salient through the meanings they entail within behavior episodes consist of behavior episode schemata containing different goals, emotions (including self-esteem), and cognitions, which, in their turn, affect behavior. This includes exercises of power that are facilitated by the activation of particular identities (Postmes & Jetten, 2006; Ford, 2013; Smith et al., 2015; Larsen & Buss, 2017; Stets & Serpe, 2017).

As they are processual and dependent on both internal processes and the social environment, identities may develop over time. Different identities that exist at the same time may be compatible or in conflict with each other. Periods of identity crisis or conflict may stimulate mental and social processes to resolve them but they may also persist (Larsen & Buss, 2017; Stets & Serpe, 2017).

Actions

The importance for individual power of the concepts described in this chapter stems from their impact on individual actions. It is through actions that individual power affects and is affected by the social environment. According to Fishbein and Ajzen's (2010) 'Reasoned Action Approach', actions follow from the information or beliefs people possess about particular actions. Such information and beliefs are seen to be influenced by interpretive and remembering processes. In light of what was discussed above, this implies that the information and beliefs an individual possesses about particular actions depend on individual goals, emotional and cognitive processes, personality traits, and salient identities.

Fishbein and Ajzen distinguish three kinds of beliefs relevant to an action: behavioral beliefs – beliefs that influence the attitude (positive or negative) toward the behavior; normative beliefs – beliefs about the extent to which important others approve or disapprove of the behavior; and control beliefs – beliefs concerning personal and environmental factors that support or impede the behavior. The attitude toward the behavior, perceived norm, and perception of behavioral control lead to the formation of an intention to perform the behavior, with the importance of the different beliefs varying depending on the behavior and the environment. The stronger the intention formed, the higher the possibility that the behavior will be performed. As Fishbein and Ajzen argue, this includes (potentially nonconscious) intentions resulting from emotional impulses or heuristics.

For the behavior to be performed, a person requires actual control over the behavior in terms of required skills and abilities and required environmental conditions. Required skills and abilities include mental capabilities that come with behavior episode schemata as supported by the neurological structuring and development of the brain. They also include physical abilities such as characteristics of a person's physiology and medical conditions, including physical health, fitness, and strength (Ford, 2013; Kandel et al., 2013; Hoffman & Knudson, 2018; Reisberg, 2018). Required environmental conditions include the absence of barriers deriving from elements of the natural environment as well as from (potential) actions by others who form the social environment. The (potential) actions by others may depend on many factors, including existing power structures, processes of exercises of power, strategies, and modalities of forms of collective power – as discussed in other chapters in this book.

Techno-adjusted individual power

Individual power may be adjusted by technologies in various ways. When technologies are made to fit the human body, this may be experienced as an adjustment of individual abilities. For conventional technologies, such as machines, tools, and vehicles, this may be achieved by means of ergonomic analysis and user-friendly design (Norman, 2013; Kroemer, 2017). Other technologies may work directly in the human body or attempt to provide interfaces that are as closely connected to the human body as possible. Technologies that have become increasingly prominent in this regard and that have a strong potential to adjust individual power are biotechnology and ICT. As defined by Khan (2020, p. 2), biotechnology involves the use of biological systems or living organisms to manufacture products or processes. For techno-adjusted individual power, the field of medical biotechnology is of particular relevance (Evens, 2020). Relevant technologies in ICT include data science and artificial intelligence systems linked to individuals through interfaces (Shah, 2020; Russell & Norvig, 2021).

According to Evens (2020), the cornerstone of biotechnology is recombinant DNA technology. In this technology, human proteins are manufactured from human genes through processes of gene isolation, cloning, and protein production. The proteins that are produced can be used to support human anatomy, physiology, and immune systems. Other types of biotechnology include monoclonal antibody technology, the production of peptides, vaccines, tissues, and liposomes, molecular engineering, gene therapy, gene editing (e.g., CRISPER), and stem cell research. Such technologies can be used to ameliorate diseases, but they can also be used to enhance functioning or performance, for instance, in sports (Van Hilvoorde, 2013; Evens, 2020; Khan, 2020).

Data science may be defined as computer-supported collecting, storing, and processing of data to derive insights that may support decision-making and actions. In this process, data may be collected from various sources such as direct input from users, logs, databases, spreadsheets, surveys, interviews, websites, and digitized publications of various kinds, after which the data is preprocessed to fit the type of analyses to be performed. Shah (2020) distinguishes exploratory, descriptive, diagnostic, predictive, prescriptive, and mechanistic (causal) analyses. In such analyses, various types of algorithmic logic may be used, of which machine learning increasingly forms a part. In machine learning, an algorithmic logic is set up that aims to match inputs to expected outputs using calibrating feedback loops. In other words, the logic of a machine learning system adjusts internal values of variables ('parameters') in the system through feedback logic so as to arrive at acceptable predictions of outputs. This logic can be used for search, classification, clustering the calculation of probabilities, determining patterns and scenarios, object recognition, speech recognition, language translation, decision-making, automated planning and scheduling, medical diagnosis, writing bots, and more. If machine learning uses many 'layers' (chunks of code with a particular machine learning function), it is referred to as 'deep learning'. If outcomes of a machine learning system resemble outcomes of an intelligent process, the system is referred to as 'artificial intelligence' (AI) (Berthold et al., 2020; Russell & Norvig, 2021).

Data science and AI systems can adjust individual power by making their functionalities and the devices/robots linked to them available to individuals through interfaces. Prime examples of such interfaces are keyboards, screens, cameras, microphones, and touchpads of computers, laptops, cell phones, and IoT devices. Other interfaces include wearable devices such as smart clothes, braces, bracelets, wrist watches, rings, glasses, headsets, and other accessories, EEG and other types of sensors of brain activity, and – currently to a very limited extent – brain implants (Nam et al., 2018; Clément, 2019; Motti, 2020; Paszkiel, 2020).

Apart from effects on individual abilities, ICT has also brought into being online identities – the ways in which users present themselves online or the ways in which the online presence of users can be interpreted in terms of identities. This includes identities on communication platforms, social platforms, government and e-commerce sites, personal websites, and in gaming communities, online meetings, online media services, and so on. Such identities may or may not have consistencies with offline identities, they may be fragmented and/or multiple, and their development may be halted and/or restarted. The extent to which possibilities for fluid or multiple online identities exist is influenced by platform policies and the amount of information available on different sites that can be linked to online and offline identities (Poletti & Rak, 2014; MacKellar, 2019).

In conclusion, where biotechnology adjusts individual power by ameliorating diseases and/or enhancing biological performance, ICT adjusts it by providing automatic information gathering and processing capabilities as well as digital identities. The empowering elements of such adjustments cannot be denied, but they are not without limitations and challenges. In biotechnology, side effects of treatments may be unknown or adverse, there is the possibility of abuse, and many techniques are still in a process of development (Evens, 2020; Khan, 2020). Applications of data science and AI depend on the systems used that tend to provide specific rather than general intelligence. In other words, these systems tend to be good at one particular thing, for example, searching websites, understanding voice commands, recognizing objects, recognizing faces, playing chess, and so on, but not at different things at the same time. The effects of data science and AI systems also depend on the effectiveness of the interfaces used, with computers currently providing higher capabilities and speed than cellphones, and much higher capabilities and speed than wearables and brain computer interfaces. In addition, the systems are highly dependent on the data, hardware, and computer skills that are used to build and calibrate them, which raises issues in terms of privacy, security, reliability of knowledge, ethics, and location, concentration, and (potential) abuse of power (Poletti & Rak, 2014; Ford, 2018; Heffernan, 2019; Khatchatourov et al., 2019; Marcus & Davis, 2019; Marcus, 2020).

Individual power and empowerment

Learning about individual power and its constituents is empowering in important ways. On the one hand, it provides an understanding of one's own individual power and how it depends on one's behavior episode schemata as these are formed during behavior episodes integrating goals, emotions, and cognitions. Combined, one's episode schemata constitute personality characteristics and identities, as well as mental skills. Together with one's physical characteristics and condition, the social environment, and techno-adjustment, this is what constitutes one's individual power. Importantly also, knowing about the constitutive elements of individual power allows for the interpretation of the individual powers of others. This not only provides an understanding of their powers but also provides access for the exercise of power – as will become apparent in the next chapter. This type of understanding is widely aimed for by marketing and human resource management analytics, with data science and AI tools providing information that can be used to interpret individual characteristics of customers and employees (Bauer et al., 2021; Venkatesan et al., 2021). Understanding the individual power of others also enhances possibilities for effective and constructive interactions in other areas of social life.

The elements of individual power described in this chapter can be used as sensitizing concepts, concepts that "suggest directions along which to look" (Blumer, 1954, p. 7). These concepts are not meant to be stable, objective, obligatory, or definitive. They are meant to serve as tools that can be used if this turns out to be helpful in interpretation. If culturally sensitive interpretation indicates that they are not helpful, they can be left out. They are meant to empower, not impede.

References

Aristotle (350 BCa). *Nichomachean ethics* (W.D. Ross, Trans.). Retrieved 2 December 2020, from http://classics.mit.edu/Aristotle/nicomachaen.mb.txt.

Aristotle (350 BCb). *Rhetoric* (W.R. Roberts, Trans.). Retrieved 2 December 2020, from http://classics.mit.edu/Aristotle/rhetoric.mb.txt.

Aristotle (350 BCc). *On the soul* (J.A. Smith, Trans.). Retrieved 2 December 2020, from http://classics.mit.edu/Aristotle/soul.mb.txt.

Baddeley A., Eysenck, M.W., & Anderson, M.C. (2014). *Memory* (2nd ed.). London: Psychology Press.

Bauer, T., Erdogan, B., Caughlin, D., & Truxillo, D. (2021). *Fundamentals of human resource management: People, data, and analytics*. Los Angeles, CA: SAGE.

Berthold, M.R., Borgelt, C., Höppner, F., Klawonn, F., & Silipo, R. (2020). *Guide to intelligent data science: How to intelligently make use of real data* (2nd ed.). Cham: Springer.

Blumer, H. (1954). What is wrong with social theory? *American Sociological Review, 19*(1), 3–10. https://doi.org/10.2307/2088165.

Bosch, R. (2012). *Wetenschapsfilosofie voor kwalitatief onderzoek*. The Hague: Boom Lemma.

Bosch, R. (2016). *Power: A conceptual analysis*. The Hague: Eleven International Publishing.

Burke, P.J. & Stets, J.E. (2009). *Identity theory*. Oxford: Oxford University Press.

Carver, C.S. (2010). Personality. In R.F. Baumeister & E.J. Finkel (Eds.), *Advanced social psychology: The state of the science* (pp. 757–794). Oxford: Oxford University Press.

Cialdini, R.B. (2009). *Influence: Science and practice* (5th ed.). Boston, MA: Pearson Education.

Clément, C. (2019). *Brain-computer interface technologies: Accelerating neuro-technology for human benefit*. Cham: Springer.

DeSteno, D., Condon, P. & Dickens, L. (2016). Gratitude and compassion. In L. Feldman Barrett, M. Lewis, & J.M. Haviland-Jones (Eds.), *Handbook of emotions* (4th ed.) (pp. 835–846). New York: The Guilford Press.

Etzioni, A. (1991). Socio-economics: A budding challenge. In A. Etzioni & P.R. Lawrence (Eds.), *Socio-economics: Toward a new synthesis* (pp. 3–7). London: M.E. Sharpe.

Evens, R.P. (2020). *Biotechnology: The science, the products, the government, the business*. London: CRC Press.

Feldman Barrett, L., Lewis, M., & Haviland-Jones, J.M. (2016). *Handbook of emotions* (4th ed.). New York: The Guilford Press.

Fishbein, M. & Ajzen, I. (2010). *Predicting and changing behavior: The reasoned action approach*. New York: Psychology Press.

Ford, D.H. (1987). *Humans as self-constructing living systems: A developmental perspective on behavior and personality*. Hillsdale, NJ: Lawrence Erlbaum.

Ford, M.E. (1992). *Motivating humans: Goals, emotions, and personal agency beliefs*. London: SAGE.

Ford, D.H. (2013). *Humans as self-constructing living systems: A developmental perspective on behavior and personality* (2nd ed.). Scotts Valley, CA: CreateSpace Independent Publishing Platform.

Ford, M. (2018). *Architects of intelligence: The truth about AI from the people building it*. Birmingham: Packt Publishing.

Frijda, N.H. & Mesquita, B. (1994). The social roles and functions of emotions. In S. Kitayama & H.R. Markus (Eds.), *Emotion and culture: Empirical studies of mutual influence* (pp. 51–87). Washington, DC: American Psychological Association.

Funder, D.C. & Fast, L.A. (2010). Personality in social psychology. In S.T. Fiske, D.T. Gilbert, & G. Lindzey (Eds.), *Handbook of social psychology* (5th ed.) (pp. 668–697). New York: Wiley.

Geertz, C. (1973). *The interpretation of cultures: Selected essays by Clifford Geertz.* New York: Basic Books.

Gilovich, T.D. & Griffin, D.W. (2010). Judgment and decision making. In S.T. Fiske, D.T. Gilbert & G. Lindzey (Eds.), *Handbook of social psychology* (5th ed.) (pp. 542–588). New York: Wiley.

Grondin, S. (2016). *Psychology of perception.* Dordrecht: Springer International Publishing.

Halpern, D.F. (2014). *Thought and knowledge: An introduction to critical thinking.* New York: Psychology Press.

Heffernan, T. (Ed.). *Cyborg futures: Cross-disciplinary perspectives on artificial intelligence and robots.* Cham: Palgrave Macmillan.

Hoffman, S.J. & Knudson, D.V. (Eds.) (2018). *Introduction to kinesiology* (5th ed.). Champaign, IL: Human Kinetics.

Homiak, M. (2019). Moral character. *The Stanford Encyclopedia of Philosophy.* Retrieved 3 December 2020, from https://plato.stanford.edu/entries/moral-character/.

Izard, C.E. (2011). Forms and functions of emotions: Matters of emotion-cognition interactions. *Emotion Review, 3*(4), 371–378. https://doi.org/10.1177/1754073911410737.

John, O.P., Naumann, L.P., & Soto, C.J. (2008). Paradigm shift to the integrative big-five trait taxonomy: History, measurement, and conceptual issues. In O.P. John, R.W. Robbins, & L.A. Pervin (Eds.), *Handbook of personality: Theory and research* (pp. 114–159). New York: Guilford Press.

Kahneman, D. (2003). A perspective on judgment and choice: Mapping bounded rationality. *American Psychologist, 58*(9), 697–720. https://doi.org/10.1037/0003-066X.58.9.697.

Kahneman, D. (2011). *Thinking fast and slow.* New York: Farrar, Straus and Giroux.

Kandel, E.R., Schwartz, J.H., Jessell, T.M., Siegelbaum, S.A., & Hudspeth, A.J. (2013). *Principles of neural science* (5th ed.). New York: McGraw-Hill Medical.

Keltner, D., Oatley, K., & Jenkins, J.M. (2013). *Understanding emotions* (3rd ed.). Hoboken, NJ: John Wiley & Sons.

Khan, F.A. (2020). *Biotechnology fundamentals* (3rd ed.). New York: CRC Press.

Khatchatourov, A., Chardel, P.-A., Feenberg, A., & Périès, A. (2019). *Digital identities in tension.* Hoboken, NJ: Wiley.

Kroemer, K.H.E. (2017). *Fitting the human: Introduction to ergonomics / human factors engineering.* New York: CRC Press.

Larsen, R. & Buss, D. (2017). *Personality psychology: Domains of knowledge about human nature* (6th ed.). New York: McGraw-Hill Education.

Machiavelli, N. (1532/2009). *The prince* (T. Parks, Trans.). London: Penguin Books.

MacKellar, C. (Ed.) (2019). *Cyborg mind: What brain-computer and mind-cyberspace interfaces mean for cyberneuroethics.* New York: Berghahn.

March, J.G. & Simon, H.A. (1993). *Organizations* (2nd ed.). Cambridge, MA: Blackwell Business.

Marcus, G. (2020). The next decade in AI. Retrieved 10 January 2021, from https://arxiv.org/ftp/arxiv/papers/2002/2002.06177.pdf.

Marcus, G. & Davis, E. (2018). *Rebooting AI: Building artificial intelligence we can trust.* New York: Pantheon Books.

Maslow, A.H. (1943). A theory of human motivation. *Psychological Review, 50*(4), 370–396. https://doi.org/10.1037/h0054346.

McCrudden, M.T. & McNamara, D.S. (2017). *Cognition in education.* New York: Routledge.

Mesquita, B. (2010). Emoting: A contextualized process. In B. Mesquita, L. Feldman Barrett, & E.R. Smith (Eds.), *The mind in context* (pp. 83–104). New York: The Guildford Press.

Mesquita, B., De Leersnyder, J., & Boiger, M. (2016). The cultural psychology of emotions. In L. Feldman Barrett, M. Lewis, & J.M. Haviland-Jones (Eds.), *Handbook of Emotions* (4th ed.) (pp. 393–411). New York: The Guilford Press.

Minda, J.P. (2015). *The psychology of thinking: Reasoning, decision-making & problem-solving.* Los Angeles, CA: SAGE.

Motti, V.G. (2020). *Wearable interaction.* Cham: Springer.

Nam, C.S., Nijholt, A., & Lotte, F. (2018). *Brain-computer interfaces handbook: Technological & theoretical advances.* London: CRC Press.

Norman, D. (2013). *The design of everyday things* (rev. & exp. ed.). New York: Basic Books.

Paszkiel, S. (2020). *Analysis and classification of EEG signals for brain-computer interfaces.* Cham: Springer.

Peirce, C.S. (1896/1931). Lessons from the history of science. In C. Hartshorne & P. Weiss (Eds.), *Collected papers of Charles Sanders Peirce. Volume 1* (pp. 43–125). Cambridge, MA: The Murray Printing Company.

Plato (375 BC). *The Republic* (B. Jowett, Trans.). Retrieved 3 December 2020, from http://classics.mit.edu/Plato/republic.mb.txt.

Poletti, A. & Rak, J. (Eds.) (2014). *Identity technologies: Constructing the self online.* Madison: The University of Wisconsin Press.

Postmes, T. & Jetten, J. (Eds.) (2006). *Individuality and the group: Advances in social identity.* London: SAGE.

Ratner, C. (2008). *Cultural psychology, cross-cultural psychology, and indigenous psychology.* New York: Nova Science Publishers.

Reisberg, D. (2018). *Cognition: Exploring the science of the mind* (7th ed.). New York: W.W. Norton & Company.

Reiss, S. (2004). Multifaceted nature of intrinsic motivation: The theory of 16 basic desires. *Review of General Psychology, 8*(3), 179–193. https://doi.org/10.1037/1089-2680.8.3.179.

Rokeach, M. (1973). *The nature of human values.* New York: The Free Press.

Russell, S. & Norvig, P. (2021). *Artificial intelligence: A modern approach* (4th ed.). Hoboken, NJ: Pearson.

Scarantino, A. (2016). The philosophy of emotions and its impact on affective Science. In L. Feldman Barrett, M. Lewis, & J.M. Haviland-Jones (Eds.), *Handbook of emotions* (4th ed.) (pp. 3–48). New York: The Guilford Press.

Schwartz, S.H. (1992). Universals in the content and structure of values: Theoretical advances and empirical tests in 20 Countries. *Advances in Experimental Psychology, 25,* 1–65. https://doi.org/10.1016/S0065-2601(08)60281-6.

Schwartz, S.H., Cieciuch, J., Vecchione, M., Davidov, E., Fischer, R., Beierlein, C., Ramos, A., Verkasalo, M.V., Lönnqvist, J.-E., Demirutku, K., Dirilen-Gumus, O., & Konty, M. (2012). Refining the theory of basic individual values. *Journal of Personality and Social Psychology, 103*(4), 663–688. https://doi.org/10.1037/a0029393.

Shah, C. (2020). *A hands-on introduction to data science.* Cambridge: Cambridge University Press.

Simon, H.A. (1979). Rational decision making in business organizations. *The American Economic Review, 69*(4), 493–513.

Smith, E.R., Mackie, D.M., & Claypool, H.M. (2015). *Social psychology* (4th ed.). New York: Psychology Press.

Sorabji, R. (2008). *Self: Ancient and modern insights about individuality, life, and death.* Chicago, IL: The University of Chicago Press.

Stets, J.E. & Serpe, R.T. (Eds.) (2017). *New directions in identity theory and research.* Oxford: Oxford University Press.

Styles, E.A. (2006). *The psychology of attention* (2nd ed.). New York: Psychology Press.

Sun, T. (6th cent. BC/1971). *The art of war* (S.B. Griffith, Trans.). Oxford: Oxford University Press.

Van Hilvoorde, I. (2013). Biotechnology. In D. Levinson & G. Pfister (Eds.), *Berkshire encyclopedia of world sport* (3rd ed.) (pp. 135–140). Great Barrington, MA: Berkshire Publishing Group.

Venkatesan, R., Farris, P.W., & Wilcox, R.T. (2021). *Marketing analytics: Essential tools for data-driven decisions.* Charlottesville, VA: Darden Business Publishing.

Vohs, K.D. & Luce, M.F. (2010). Judgment and decision making. In R.F. Baumeister & E.J. Finkel (Eds.), *Advanced social psychology: The state of the science* (pp. 733–756). Oxford: Oxford University Press.

Watt Smith, T. (2016). *The book of human emotions: From ambiguphobia to umpty -154 words from around the world for how we feel.* New York: Little, Brown and Company.

Zaki, J. & Ochsner, K. (2016). Empathy. In L. Feldman Barrett, M. Lewis, & J.M. Haviland-Jones (Eds.), *Handbook of emotions* (4th ed.) (pp. 871–884). New York: The Guilford Press.

Zimbardo, P.G. & Leippe, M.R. (1991). *The psychology of attitude change and social influence.* New York: McGraw-Hill.

4

EXERCISING POWER

Chapter 2 discussed the distribution of relative abilities in structures of power, and Chapter 3 the way in which relative abilities may constitute individual power. In this chapter, the focus shifts to how such relative abilities can be used to exercise power. An exercise of power can be aimed at oneself, including such activities as eating, drinking, exercising, studying, and so on. It may also be aimed at nature, ranging from activities such as throwing rocks or riding a horse, to building, engineering, and production. Finally, an exercise of power can be aimed at other people, and this will be the focus of this chapter. There is a multitude of ways in which an exercise of power can be aimed at other people. Broadly speaking, a distinction can be drawn between exercises of power that do not specifically aim to change other people's psychological characteristics, and exercises of power that do. The first type of exercise of power includes such social control processes as force, coercion, certain forms of manipulation, and the use of authority. The second type of power includes ways of legitimation and various types of social influence.

This chapter will describe various social control, legitimation, and social influence techniques. Learning about such techniques can be particularly empowering – first and foremost because it allows for the recognition of when and how such techniques are being used by others so that strategies can be considered to respond to them. The development and implementation of strategies will be discussed in the next chapter. Learning about social control, legitimation, and social influence techniques also provides knowledge of how to use these techniques oneself. This raises complex ethical issues. The position taken here is that the more people learn about ways in which power can be exercised over others, the higher the chance may be that such techniques are used constructively rather than abusively, simply because more people will recognize the techniques being used which allows them to respond strategically.

DOI: 10.4324/9781003034100-5

Force

'Force' will here be defined as physical activity directed at other people's bodies or properties. This includes activities that inflict injury or damage, such as killing, hitting, torturing, raping, bombing, removing, destroying, burning, stealing, or sabotaging. These, and their unsuccessful attempts, will here be referred to as 'violence'. Force also includes such physical activities as construction work, providing care, policing, and practicing sports.

Machiavelli (1532/2009) argued that violence can be used successfully to attain power and secure positions, but in order to do so, it needs to be applied instantly and decisively. If it is continued longer than necessary, it is expected to stir up hostility. In Machiavelli's view, once a desired position of power has been reached, it should be used to deliver benefits to those subject to it, rather than to continue using violence. Arendt (1969, p. 53) too saw violence as providing "the most effective command, resulting in the most instant and perfect obedience". According to Arendt, the effectiveness of violence depends on popular support, and this implies that it can only be used to reach short-term goals. This is because if violence persists, it will undermine popular support and stimulate others to use it as well. And when violence no longer receives popular support, it is thought to only lead to destruction.

More generally, the exercise of violence may eliminate possibilities and lead to fear in subjects, thereby supporting structures of power. It may also make other exercises of power such as coercion and social influence more effective by supporting the threat of additional violence. Furthermore, by using violence against some, others may be deterred from noncompliance. And a use of violence against a common enemy may effectively support a position of power. But the use of violence requires a lot of resources and efforts, especially if it is ineffective and needs to be repeated. The situation it imposes tends to be provisional and it may provoke resistance and counterviolence. It may create martyrs, and commands to use it may be disobeyed (Bachrach & Baratz, 1963; Lenski, 1966; Lukes, 1995; Archer, 1996; Poggi, 2001; Bosch, 2016).

The term 'violence' has been applied more widely than in reference to physical violence only. Not only has it been used to refer to the use of abusive language, which may support intimidation and undermine authority (Arendt, 1969), it has also been applied to other ways in which language may affect others with effects that are thought of or experienced as damaging (Rae & Ingala, 2018). In this chapter, the latter will be discussed in terms of other concepts which more or less cover similar conceptual territory, including legitimation and social influence techniques.

Non-violent, constructive uses of force also exist. These include such exercises of power as construction work, providing care, policing, and practicing sports. It may seem straightforward to mention such uses of force, but due to general connotations of the notion of power, such references are often missing in the power debate. Still it is important to note that while force, like other exercises of power, may be used abusively, it may, and often is, used in a constructive, empowering manner.

Force is often included as a part of strategy, for instance by Sun (6th cent. BC/1971), Von Clausewitz (1832/1989), and others. This will be discussed in the next chapter which deals with strategy. In addition, force is often exercised in and by organizations and social groups. This will be discussed in Chapter 6 which focuses on collective power.

Coercion

'Coercion' can be defined as the securing of compliance of another or others by means of the threat or application of negative sanctions (Lukes, 1995). This includes the threat of the use of force, as when someone is threatened with a weapon or physical force. But threats may also be based on economic sanctions such as withholding financial resources or employment, legal sanctions of various kinds, or social/norm-related sanctions such as contempt, ridicule, or ousting. Threats and sanctions may be expressed in various ways, including intimidation, physical removal, blackmail, confiscation, boycotts, surveillance, fines, censorship, discrimination, segregation, and shaming (Lukes, 1995; Poggi, 2001; Bosch, 2016).

Sun (6th cent. BC/1971) argued that for negative sanctions to be moral, they need to be consistent, reasonable, and applied when deserved. Machiavelli (1532/2009) warned that negative sanctions should be applied only in such a manner as to not provoke revenge. If coercion is to be effective, those subject to it must be aware of it and understand what compliance and the negative sanctions entail. The threat of sanctions also needs to be credible. But the awareness and understanding that are required for coercion to work may lead to defiance. It may make subjects recognize that alternatives to compliance are in fact available. It may also require a lot of effort and/or resources to coerce others into doing something they do not want to do (Lukes, 1995; Archer, 1996; Bosch, 2016).

It may be difficult to see how an act of coercion could be empowering by itself. But coercion can be used in self-defense or in defense of others, and it often is. This may take the form of rules that serve to defend oneself or others. Rules, whether in the form of formal rules such as laws or in the form of social norms, tend to combine coercion with inducement as will be discussed in the next section.

Manipulation

Lukes (1995, p. 10) defined manipulation as "the securing of compliance of another or others by the strategic use of an art or skill". It may specifically aim to change people's psychological characteristics, in which case it constitutes a form of social influence which will be discussed in a subsequent section. Several forms of manipulation have been distinguished that do not specifically aim to change other people's psychological characteristics, including inducement, divide and conquer, and deception. These forms of manipulation aim to alter situations so as to change the attractiveness of different courses of action.

In inducement, rewards are provided in exchange for compliance (Parsons, 1963). What constitutes a reward depends on the situation and those involved. Obvious examples include money, promotions, co-optations, prizes, praises, and so on. According to Sun (6th cent. BC/1971), for inducement to be effective, rewards should be clear and not excessive. Machiavelli (1532/2009) argued that rewards should be given out slowly and predictably. Inducement can be effective and reliable, but only as long as rewards are regularly provided, and this requires adequate resources to do so (Scott, 2001).

Inducement can be used together with coercion, and this may take the form of formal or informal rules that privilege certain types of behavior while constraining others. Formal rules are supported by existing political power structures, exercises of force, coercion, and inducement, and/or support from public opinion. When they are transgressed, repressive sanctions of various kinds may be inflicted, including physical punishment, economic fines, transfer, demotion, layoff, restraining orders, or the duty to perform certain actions such as refunding, providing compensatory services, undergoing therapy, or participating in courses. Informal rules, such as social norms, habits, customs, and moral codes, are based on social expectations, approval, and disapproval. These may have traditional or rational grounds, but they may also be influenced by normalizing effects of scientific measurements, claims to objectivity, technologies for planning, evaluation, surveillance, control, and production, requirements for transparency, accountability, and audit, and the organization of physical space. Adherence to informal rules is supported by social rewards such as praise or positions of status, whereas transgression is punished through shaming, derogation, or expulsion (Russell, 1938; Etzioni, 1968; Foucault, 1982, 2003; Powell, 1991; Clegg & Haugaard, 2009; Ryan, 2009; Sayer, 2012; Bosch, 2016).

"When he is united, divide him", Sun (6th cent. BC/1971, p. 69) wrote in *The Art of War*, which may be one of the earliest written sources of the idea of exercising power through divide and conquer. This idea can also be found in Aristotle's *The Politics* (350 BCa), where Aristotle notes that a way to preserve a tyranny is "to stir up strife and set friends against friends, people against notables and the rich against each other". It was also suggested by Machiavelli (1521/2003, p. 187) in his book *Art of War*, where he wrote that "a captain ought with every art to contrive to divide the forces of his enemy". Such a division of powers may entail the fragmentation of structures of power, the separation of activities, or the division of systems of rules, competences, interests, and processes of collective power (Poggi, 2001; Bosch, 2016). Implementations of divide and conquer include the separation of powers of government to impede centralized political power as suggested by Montesquieu (1748/1989), and the enforcement of market competition to counter centralized economic power (Letwin, 1954). As an exercise of power, divide and conquer relies on other ways of exercising power, such as force, coercion, inducement, or one of the other ways of exercising power described in this chapter, to attain its result.

On the use of deception, Sun wrote the following:

> All warfare is based on deception. Therefore, when capable, feign incapacity; when active, inactivity. When near, make it appear that you are far away; when far away, that you are near.
>
> *(Sun, 6th cent. BC/1971, p. 66)*

Two millennia later, Machiavelli also emphasized the importance of deception, lying, and hypocrisy for power:

> a ruler... must seem and sound wholly compassionate, wholly loyal, wholly humane, wholly honest and wholly religious.... The crowd is won over by appearances and final results. And the world is all crowd: the dissenting few find no space so long as the majority have any grounds at all for their opinions.
>
> *(Machiavelli, 1532/2009, p. 71)*

Not only may deception be used to hide one's actual power, activities, location, or motives, it may also be used in the hiding, mystifying, distorting, devaluation, or naturalization of ideas and depictions of situations (Morgan, 1986; Archer, 1996). A specific type of deception is the use of secret agents or spies who deceive others by hiding their identities or presence. According to Sun, the use of spies is essential to attain power. As he wrote in his chapter dedicated to the employment of secret agents:

> the reason the enlightened prince and the wise general conquer the enemy... is foreknowledge.... 'foreknowledge'... must be obtained from men who know the enemy situation.
>
> *(Sun, 6th cent. BC/1971, pp. 144–145)*

Other types of manipulation include 'heresthetic' – the structuring of voting situations through agenda control, strategic voting, or the redirection of attention; the use of timing, visibility, or symbols to direct attention; and the definition of enemies (Morgan, 1986; Lukes, 1995; Torfing, 2009; Bosch, 2016).

The use of authority

Power may be exercised through the use of authority to issue commands. In such a case, obedience to commands results from the belief that the commands derive from a legitimate source, that they were arrived at through a legitimate procedure, or that the commands themselves are legitimate (Engelstad, 2009; Beetham, 2013). As was discussed in Chapter 2, such beliefs in legitimacy of authority may result from the believed legality of rules, traditions, charisma, norms, expertise, or recognition. They may also result from legitimation or social influence processes which will be discussed later in this chapter. In the use of authority, legitimacy can be inferred on the basis of various symbols. These may range from wealth, status, position, credentials, competences, and knowledge, to existing networks and reputations for power (Lukes, 1995; Hobbes, 1651/1996; Machiavelli, 1532/2009; Bosch, 2016). In contrast to force and coercion, the use of authority is a relatively reliable way of exercising power, as long as the source of authority and the commands given remain legitimate (Beetham, 2013).

The use of technology in social control

Technologies can play an important role in social control techniques. Examples include technologies embodied in weapons, machines, tools, biological and medical substances, infrastructure, and architecture, which be used in various ways in force, coercion, and/or manipulation. In a general sense, technologies embodied in artifacts and artificial processes and systems can enhance the effectiveness and efficiency of social control (Latour, 2005; Brey, 2008).

In the exercise of force, artifacts may be used directly on another person's body or properties. This happens, for instance, when weapons are used in direct violence, physical support is provided to someone using an artifact, or tools are used in construction or destruction. The effect of such a direct exercise of force may continue in time if the artifact has a continuing forcing effect, as, for instance, torture and constraining artifacts may have (Winner, 1980; Brey, 2008). As a result of intervening artificial processes and systems, there may also be a considerable distance in space and/or time between the instigation of force and its effects. Such intervening processes and systems may range from simple machines to communication networks and data science and AI based systems. In the extreme case, AI based systems exerting force may operate without further human intervention after having been activated, as in autonomous weapon systems (AWS) also sometimes referred to as killer robots (Krishnan, 2009; Department of Defense, 2012; Pasquale, 2020).

Artifacts that may be used in force may also be used as a threat or as support for negative sanctions in coercion. In addition, they can be used to structure situations so as to make certain types of behavior difficult, painful, or unpleasant, *de facto* imposing sanctions if those behaviors are performed. Examples include the use of infrastructure, architecture, or product design to coerce certain types of behavior (Brey, 2008). The possibility to use artifacts in on- and offline surveillance has increased significantly due to developments in electronic equipment and ICT. Sensors, networks, computers, and data storage centers can collect massive amounts of data, and store and share them. Artificial processes and systems based on data science and AI allow for the linking and analysis of data, object and facial recognition, profiling, predictive policing, censoring, and raising alarm, limited by information integration, communications, computational, security, legal, and ethical issues. These electronic and ICT systems, sometimes referred to as the 'information panopticon', can be used to evaluate in detail whether or not certain behaviors are in line with formal and informal rules. Positive incentives can be automatically created for behaviors that are in line with the rules, as can punishments for behaviors that deviate from the rules. The application of such incentives and punishments can be made public to a wide audience using ICT tools, thereby strengthening their effects (Zuboff, 1988; Fogg, 2002; Perry & Roda, 2017; Chen et al., 2018; Yan, 2019; Pasquale, 2020; Sewell, 2021).

When surveillance equipment, processes, and systems are linked to positive incentives, they are used in a manipulative manner. Other types of artifacts may also be used manipulatively when they link incentives to certain types of behaviors, cause divisions between people, or have or allow for deceptive effects (Fogg, 2002; Brey, 2008). The internet, as a network artifact, supports the fast and large-scale dissemination of deceptive information that has been referred to as fake news. In addition, the flow of information on social media sites is filtered by AI algorithms that are often based on user preferences, thereby supporting one-sided views. The rise of deep fakes produced by AI algorithms further contributes to possibilities for deception (Greifeneder et al., 2021; McBrayer, 2021). Other types of deception on the internet include hacking attempts such as phishing, cross-site scripting, the use of malware such as key-loggers, viruses, trojans, and worms, form-, crypto-, and clickjacking, and providing fake wireless access points (Symantec, 2019).

Artifacts can be used to express authority, when the source responsible for the artifact is recognized as legitimate. In such a case, the artifacts carry symbolic meanings that serve as authoritative commands, as, for instance, traffic lights do. Websites may attain credibility that may support the use of personal information and financial transactions (Fogg, 2002; Brey, 2008).

Legitimation

Using authority is one thing, establishing authority is another. The latter may be referred to as 'legitimation' – the process in which attempts are made to convince others that structures of power, procedures, commands, processes, actions, and/or obedience are rightful. Such legitimation can take the form of various uses of language, such as the construction of conceptions of reality and social categories through discourse, the presentation of ideologies, theories, and/or myths, and justifications in terms of traditions, rules, or charisma. Other forms of legitimation include the use of symbols and rituals (Bosch, 2016).

According to Foucault (1975/1977), discourses as systems of meaning determine what can and cannot be said, what is normal and deviant, true and false, reasonable and unreasonable. The communication that results is seen to reinforce and legitimate knowledge claims that are contained in accepted, normal, true, and reasonable discourses. In their turn, legitimated knowledge claims support political power, as was noted in Chapter 2. Adherents of different discourses may attempt to broaden the acceptance of their discourses with the identities, values, norms, patterns of actions, and legitimate knowledge claims that are connected to them, potentially aiming to achieve hegemony (Gramsci, 1971; Bosch, 2016).

Discourses convey and are underpinned by ideologies – sets of political beliefs and values that guide behavior. Ideologies influence how the world is viewed, providing a shared set of values and beliefs to their adherents. In doing so, they legitimize particular structures of power, patterns of behavior, emotional commitments, and interests (Mannheim, 1929/1936; Poggi, 2001; Bosch, 2016; Flowerdew & Richardson, 2018). In an elaborate categorization of ideologies, Heywood (2017) distinguishes liberalism, conservatism, socialism, anarchism, nationalism, fascism, feminism, green ideology, multiculturalism, and Islamism. According to this categorization, liberalism promotes individual freedom, fulfilment, rationality, equal rights, and tolerance; conservatism emphasizes tradition, human imperfection, hierarchy, authority, and property; socialism values community, cooperation, equality of outcome, and common ownership; anarchism is characterized by anti-statism, natural order, anti-clericalism, and economic freedom; nationalism promotes the nation, organic community, self-determination, and culturalism; fascism champions anti-rationalism, struggle, leadership, elitism, socialism, and ultranationalism; feminism addresses themes such as the personal, patriarchy, sex and gender, and gender equality and difference; green ideology centers around ecology, holism, sustainability, environmental ethics, and well-being; multiculturalism endorses political recognition, pride in culture and identity, minority rights, and diversity; and Islamism emphasizes fundamentalism, a revolt against the West, the construction of an Islamic state, and jihadism. These ideologies are seen to contain various sub-traditions and they may be combined in diverse hybrid forms. Other ideologies have been distinguished, including Christian democracy, social democracy, communism, libertarianism, populism, republicanism, ideologies of empire, and various ideologies specific to Africa, China, and South and Southeast Asia (Freeden et al., 2015).

Ideologies or parts of them may be constructed or expanded for legitimation purposes. This can be done by linking new or additional ideas to ideas that are already accepted and taken for granted. The scope of application of an ideology can be expanded by adjusting structures of power, patterns of action, or psychological commitments to fit the ideology. Once in existence, ideologies can be used in processes of indoctrination. Such processes imply exposing people to ideological ideas while limiting the exposure of, or criticizing alternative ideas (Skinner, 1988; Tully, 1988; Poggi, 2001).

Ideologies can support elaborate systems of structures of power, but the use of ideas in legitimation may also be more specific. It can take the form of justifications in terms of rules, as when reference is made to legal or organizational rules as defined by authoritative sources. It may also be based on references to traditional ideas, precedents, established characteristics of reference groups, or publications from traditional sources. Charisma can be used, in the form of pretenses or demonstrations of status, strength, achievement, wealth, powerful networks, and exemplary actions. References may be made to accepted norms, expertise, or recognition by authoritative parties (Poggi, 2001; Engelstad, 2009; Haugaard & Clegg, 2009; Beetham, 2013; Bosch, 2016).

Legitimation can also occur by means of myths that take the form of legitimating stories. Such stories may be concerned with such subjects as the divine right to rule, the rule of the majority, the burdens and benefits of rule, equality between rulers and ruled, the danger of enemies, heroism, freedom, nature, science, truth, or religion, and superiority of rulers in terms of character, intellect, and wealth. In the process of legitimation, mythical stories may be composed in such a way that they aim to effect particular authorities (Poggi, 2001; Engelstad, 2009; Machiavelli, 1532/2009; Beetham, 2013; Segal, 2015; Bosch, 2016).

Yet another approach to legitimation is the use of symbols, ranging from banners and slogans to dress codes, decorations, prizes, types of architecture, physical layouts, the use of titles, sacred texts, and more. Such symbols may aim to evoke sentiments that support authority, such as feelings of pride, allegiance, and trust. They can also serve to include and exclude, legitimating what is included or excluded. Religious symbols can legitimate structures of power as sacred or divine, and oppose what is considered to be profane (; Bourdieu, 1979/1984; Poggi, 2001; Engelstad, 2009; Bosch, 2016).

A ritual may be defined as a stylized, regularly repeated social occasion "where participants recapitulate an ancient event, a common loyalty or a relationship to a deity" (Engelstad, 2009, p. 213). It can be used as a legitimation technique by modeling and representing structures of power and stimulating the identification of participants with values contained in the ritual. Examples of rituals that may legitimate power include initiations, rites of passage, processions, parades, ceremonies, communal singing, holiday celebrations, and religious practices (Van Gennep, 1908/1960; Turner, 1967; Handelman, 1990; Grimes, 2013; Stephenson, 2015).

Social influence

As stated in the introduction to this chapter, the term social influence will here be used to refer to exercises of power that specifically aim to change other people's psychological characteristics. Social influence utilizes aspects of the processes of attention, goals, emotions, thinking, identity, and actions that were described in Chapter 3.

Social influence through attention

People can only attend to a limited amount of information at once. This characteristic of the attention process is used as a first step in various social influence techniques. In such techniques, people are selectively exposed to particular items of information in order to activate specific behavior episode schemata. These activated behavior episode schemata are then capitalized upon in various ways.

One such capitalization is the attempt to establish recognition or liking through repeated exposure. Another is the attempt to make certain items of information more influential than others by presenting them at the beginning of an attention process, thereby establishing a primacy effect, or at the end, establishing a recency effect (Fishbein & Ajzen, 1975; Zimbardo & Leippe, 1991; Kahneman, 2011; Bosch, 2016).

Exposure to an item that activates particular behavior episode schemata may be repeatedly linked to exposure to another item. This may lead the second item to activate the same behavior episode schemata by itself, a process referred to as classical conditioning. This way, the item may take over negative or positive evaluative properties of the first item, an effect that is often aspired to in, for instance, marketing and propaganda. The span of someone's attention may also be used to provide an example of behavior in order to achieve what is known as observational learning. At the same time, attention may be distracted away from unwanted sources of influence (Bandura, 1986; Petty & Briñol, 2010; Bosch, 2016).

Social influence through human goals

Once attention has been achieved, social influence can be directed at other aspects of behavior episode schemata in order to achieve change. One component of behavior episode schemata, as described in Chapter 3, consists of human goals. By linking objects, ideas, or actions to human goals people aspire to, social influence techniques can aim to change evaluations of such objects, ideas, or actions. This can be done in various ways, some of which will be described in this section.

Social influence may aim to relate to the goals of power, status, and achievement people may have by linking objects, ideas, or actions to powerful, high status, successful, or glamorous people or outcomes, this way establishing positive evaluations. Appearances of luxury, expensiveness, heroism, or possibilities at self-aggrandizement or self-gratification can provide a similar influencing effect. People with the goal of curiosity may be related to by claiming that objects, ideas, or actions that are attended to are novel or creative, a technique often used in marketing and political speeches. An attempt can be made to connect to people with independence or self-direction goals by linking objects, ideas, or actions to the idea that these enhance or limit freedom. This may lead to positive or negative evaluations – where negative evaluation may activate the goal of vengeance (Zimbardo & Leippe, 1991; Bosch, 2016). The connection to self-direction also plays a role in the 'principle of scarcity' posited by Cialdini (2009), according to which opportunities seem more valuable when they are less available, which stimulates particular actions such as buying.

The goals of honor, idealism, benevolence, and universalism play a role in the principle of reciprocation, which states that one should repay what another person has provided. Appealing to people with these goals by providing what seems to constitute a gift or free service can activate reciprocation behavior, as is often done with the provision of samples of products or customer service (Cialdini, 2009). Other social influence techniques relating to these goals may present objects, ideas, or actions as honorable, ethical, or 'God's will', potentially leading to changed attitudes or beliefs. The goal of physical exercise can be connected to objects, ideas, or actions by linking them to activities such as sports and health, making those objects, ideas, or actions more attractive to those for whom this goal is important. Social influence techniques may relate to people with the goals of romance, eating, stimulation, and/or hedonism by connecting objects, ideas, or actions to fun, good food, sex, intimacy, or tenderness (Zimbardo & Leippe, 1991; Bosch, 2016).

People with the goals of order, social contact, acceptance, face, tradition, and conformity may be appealed to by linking the presentation of objects, ideas, or actions to the idea that these are socially approved. These goals play a central role in the principles of social proof and commitment and consistency distinguished by Cialdini (2009). According to the principle of social proof, people decide what is correct by finding out what similar people think is correct, which implies that their beliefs may be changed according to what they find. Commitment and consistency refers to personal and interpersonal pressures to behave consistently with prior commitments, which may result in desired behaviors. Other social influence techniques focusing on these goals include the use of references to etiquette, morality, and responsibility, all aiming to influence attitudes, beliefs, or actions by means of such referencing (Bosch, 2016).

Presenting objects, ideas, or actions as comfortable, convenient, or easy relates to people with the goal of tranquility (Zimbardo & Leippe, 1991; Kahneman, 2011). The goal of security can be related to when presenting objects, ideas, or actions as providing safety and protection, or alternatively, as having adverse effects on safety (Lukes, 1995; Bosch, 2016). Here again, the activation of these goals aims to change the evaluations of the presented objects, ideas, or actions that are linked to the goals in a desired direction.

Social influence through emotions

Social influence techniques may aim to evoke emotions and link them to presented objects, people, ideas, or actions. This way, changes in evaluation, thinking, or behavior may be effected. Again, as in the case of human goals, the possibilities to do this are manifold. The discussion here will be limited to some salient ones.

The emotions of interest and surprise can be evoked by presenting something as different or new. Thus, presenting familiar objects, ideas, or actions as improved or new can stimulate renewed interest – as is often done in marketing and politics. The emotion of joy can be appealed to by using themes of hope or optimism, a technique often used in political speeches. Sexual arousal can be evoked by presenting sexual imagery or sounds – the classic example of which being that of scantily dressed women standing next to expensive cars to induce buying behavior. Attempts may be made to link objects, ideas, or actions to affective emotions such as love, liking, and trust by connecting them to pleasant music, good food, popular organizations, people, or symbols, or to (pretenses of) agreeableness, warmth, esthetics, trustworthiness, authority, and status. Excitement and awe can be elicited by stimulating presentations, spectacles, and festivities, again supporting particular ideas or behaviors linked to such elicitations (Zimbardo & Leippe, 1991; Cialdini, 2009; Bosch, 2016).

The evocation of negative emotions such as shame or guilt through assigning blame can activate feelings of the need for reciprocation. Anger or fear can be evoked and capitalized upon in attempts to channel beliefs and actions in directions desired by influencing parties. Negative attitudes toward objects, people, ideas, or actions can be aroused by linking them to negative emotions such as disgust, contempt, jealousy, or envy. Social influence techniques may also be based on countering negative emotions by promising relief, security, and reassurance, all in the attempt of affecting attitudes, beliefs, and behaviors (Zimbardo & Leippe, 1991; Bosch, 2016).

Social influence through thinking

When social influence aims to change or strengthen feelings, ideas, or actions through the thinking process, it may aim at System 1 or System 2 – as described in Chapter 3. When aimed at System 1 (fast thinking), heuristics are activated in order to achieve the desired change. To achieve change by addressing System 2 (slow thinking), social influence is based on persuasion.

Heuristics that were summarized in Chapter 3 may be activated in several ways. The order in which items are presented may lead to priming, a recency effect, intensity matching, activation of the law of small numbers, and/or anchoring. Information may be provided selectively in an attempt to direct or strengthen existing ideas or behaviors – capitalizing on confirmation bias and availability. The halo effect can be activated by linking ideas or actions to a likeable item. To activate the representativeness heuristic, analogies or metaphors may be used. Information may be presented that seems plausible, contains a causal argument, or appears to be based on correlation, even if the information is not statistically probable. Hindsight bias may be capitalized upon in attempts to attain acceptability of surprising information. In parallel processes, outcome bias may help in making outcomes acceptable regardless of the process that led to them, and inconsistencies in the application of criteria can be used to reach acceptability of information that might not be so according to those criteria. Loss aversion may be activated in others to reap related gains for oneself (Kahneman, 2011).

Cialdini (2009) distinguished six heuristics activated in social influence techniques. The heuristic of reciprocation can be activated by inducing a sense of obligation in someone through gift giving, the 'door-in-the-face' technique (following a large request with a smaller one to be reciprocated), and the 'that's-not-all' technique (improving a proposal to stimulate reciprocation). This way, desired reciprocations can be incited. The heuristic of commitment and consistency can be invoked by the 'foot-in-the-door' technique (making a small request first, followed by a larger one), the 'low-balling' technique (making an attractive offer first, followed by a lesser one), and having people make public statements. The heuristic of social proof can be used by providing examples produced by members of reference groups people aspire to belong to. The liking heuristic allows for influence through feelings of liking similar to the halo effect described earlier. The heuristic of authority refers to the use of symbols of authority to attain conformity, as described above in the section on the use of authority. Finally, the scarcity heuristic can be activated by claiming that certain items are scarce – as is often done in marketing.

Social influence techniques may also aim to arouse psychological reactance by claiming infringements exist on someone's freedom or interests. The choice of a particular alternative can be made more appealing through use of the attraction heuristic (by introducing a new possibility to which the desired alternative compares favorably); by using the compromise heuristic (where a desired option is introduced as a compromise between two alternatives); or by presenting a desired option as a possibility to diversify (Cialdini, 2009; Bosch, 2016).

When social influence aims at System 2, methods of persuasion can be used that aim to convince others through argumentation. For this to be effective, people need to be exposed and pay attention to the arguments that are presented. Next, they have to understand the arguments, become convinced by them, and (potentially) act in accordance with them. To some extent, the legitimation techniques that were described earlier form a special case of persuasion, and elements that are used in legitimation can be used in other forms of persuasion. This includes the construction of social categories through discourse, and the use of ideologies, theories, myths, tradition, rules, charisma, symbols, and rituals. Where legitimation aims to convince others of the existence of authority, social influence may use similar elements to convince others of particular ideas or affect their behaviors.

In his book *Rhetoric*, Aristotle (350 BCb) argued that the process of persuasion starts with looking for available means of persuasion. The persuasiveness of arguments next depends most importantly on establishing credibility of the speaker ('ethos'), arousing emotions in the audience ('pathos'), and providing proof or apparent proof ('logos') through empirical examples or, more powerfully, through the use of clear, concise, and valid logical deductions ('enthymemes') that fit beliefs held by the audience. The relative emphasis on these elements depends on the right timing ('kairos'). Desired beliefs or behaviors should be depicted as good and undesired beliefs or behaviors as bad. The most important arguments should be stated in the beginning, and the use of metaphors, euphemisms, analogies, and stories are thought to enhance persuasiveness (Eyman, 2015; Kraus, 2015; Hall, 2018). Cicero (84–44 BC/2016) extended Aristotle's ideas by arguing that effective persuasion also requires wide and deep knowledge of the subject matter, an ordered arrangement of the message, a clear, correct, appropriate, and embellished style, memorization of the order of arguments and the substance of the proofs to be provided, and effective delivery.

These classical ideas on rhetoric have been elaborated upon in various ways. According to Toulmin's (2003) courtroom model, keeping in mind possible conditions of rebuttal to arguments as well as an interpreting neutral third party, helps in tailoring arguments to an audience. Arguments need to be consistent with assumptions held by an audience ('warrants'), or arguments need to be provided to establish required assumptions ('backing'). Empirical evidence ('grounds') needs to be provided to support the arguments made. When empirical evidence is not very strong, a qualification of arguments may help (Ramage et al., 2015). In addition to these ideas, it has been argued that arguments may be more convincing if the provided evidence is sufficient, representative, accurate, and relevant, if the word 'because' is used before presenting a causal statement, and if attention to opposing arguments is distracted. The use of framing – presenting arguments in such a way as to invoke specific contextual interpretive perspectives – may support effective persuasion, as may the use of themes, such as optimism, novelty, confidence, quality, inevitability, or, with reverse effects, perversity or obsoleteness (Goffman, 1986; Lukes, 1995; Cialdini, 2009; Kahneman, 2011; Ramage et al., 2015).

When the aim is to change behavior, persuasion needs to aim at changing attitudes to the behavior and subjective norms so as to change intentions. To change attitudes, specific beliefs and/or evaluations with regard to the behavior need to be changed. Subjective norms can be changed by influencing specific normative beliefs and the willingness to comply with them. The latter can be done by means of social proof, that is, by arguing that members of valued reference groups hold such norms and behave accordingly (Fishbein & Ajzen, 2010).

Social influence through identity

In a social influence process, information may be provided that is claimed to be consistent with a person's identity. Appearances may be created with desired identities, by connecting information to visions of how people may want to see themselves – for instance, as young, energetic, tough, serious, sophisticated, or gentle. This way, such information may become accepted more easily. Brand images may also be created that appear to fit particular ideas about identity, stimulating buying behaviors (Zimbardo & Leippe, 1991; Cialdini, 2009; Bosch, 2016; Clegg et al., 2019).

Influencers may aim to enhance their influence by claiming to be similar to others in terms of their identities, by using such words as 'we', 'us', 'they', or 'them', the symbolic names for particular identities, or by using symbols or behaviors connected to specific identities. Categorizing labels or other kinds of symbols may be used as a means of defining and ascribing identities, as may the allocation of roles, or the use of various types of discourse. This can be used to achieve group formation and direction or, alternatively, as a technique of divide and conquer. Information may be presented in an attempt to change a person's identity, as when questions are asked that may bring those answering the questions to see themselves differently (Zimbardo & Leippe, 1991; Cialdini, 2009; Engelstad, 2009; Haslam et al., 2011).

Social influence techniques can aim at members of groups that provide identities, thereby activating group pressures. Categorization of people into groups can by itself lead to an accentuation of differences with perceived out-groups. Influencing group members with a high status in the group may effect changes in the group as a whole, thereby affecting identities provided by the group (Paulus, 1989; Bosch, 2016).

Social influence through behavior

Social influence through behavior occurs when subtle situational pressures evoke particular behaviors which subsequently effect cognitive changes. This may take several forms, including those working through social learning, obedience, conformity, and active participation or role playing. In a process of social learning, small inducements or punishments are given to stimulate particular behaviors that, once performed, turn out to be difficult to justify in terms of the small inducements or punishments themselves. This leads to cognitive dissonance – a mismatch between the cognitions of having performed the behaviors and those providing justifications for those behaviors. Because cognitive dissonance feels uncomfortable, it can lead to changes in cognitions. As the cognitions of having performed the behavior cannot change, there will be an urge to change the justifications for the behaviors in the direction aimed for in the social influence process (Festinger, 1954; Zimbardo & Leippe, 1991; Fishbein & Ajzen, 2010; Bosch, 2016). In a process of obedience, direct requests lead to compliant behaviors because rewards or punishments are expected otherwise, or because compliance offers an escape from an uncomfortable situation. If the performed behaviors are subsequently attributed to the self rather than to external causes, this can lead to changes in justifications for the behaviors (Zimbardo & Leippe, 1991; Bosch, 2016).

The use of conformity in social influence entails an attempt to change beliefs or behaviors by creating or suggesting the existence of group pressures. Such group pressures may be normative, which means that the change in beliefs or behaviors are (claimed to be) necessary to attain positive affect from the group. They may also be informational, which implies that social comparison suggests the particular change in beliefs or behaviors (Deutsch & Gerard, 1955; Zimbardo & Leippe, 1991; Bosch, 2016). The use of active participation in social influence implies making people act out particular ideas, patterns of behavior, or roles, leading to changes in cognitions. Role-playing may entail a need to develop beliefs and/or behaviors that fit and support a particular role. This works most effectively when the role-playing is felt to be voluntary, though forced role-playing can also be effective (Zimbardo & Leippe, 1991; Fishbein & Ajzen, 2010; Petty & Briñol, 2010; Bosch, 2016).

The use of technology in legitimation and social influence

Artifacts and artificial processes and systems can legitimate authority. The symbolic meanings attached to artifacts may lend authority to those who possess or do not possess them. The symbolic meanings of artifacts can also provide legitimation to particular discourses, ideologies, or myths. This does not only hold for artifacts that serve to express symbolic meanings, it also holds for artifacts that are of practical use, and that by offering such practical use provide legitimacy. Examples are an AI-based recommendation engine that provides authority to a particular type of behavior, or a solar panel that by means of its successful operation provides legitimacy to green ideology. Reversely, authority may be established for artifacts or artificial systems by linking them to real life authorities such as doctors, teachers, or 'deep learners' (Fogg, 2002; Brey, 2008).

The possibility to exercise social influence through technology has become particularly prominent in ICT. Many of these social influence techniques have similarities to the social influence techniques described earlier in this chapter, but, as noted by Fogg (2002, p. 7), computers have certain characteristics that potentially enhance their effectiveness: they are more persistent, may offer the appearance of anonymity, can handle large volumes of data, can use many different ways to influence at the same time, allow for the large-scale application of social influence, and they may work directly on individuals through their access to interfaces close to homes and bodies.

Websites can attempt to direct people's attention with attractive and user-friendly designs in order to seduce people to click on or select items, as in online shopping. The effectiveness of such an attempt can be enhanced by making items highly visible, providing feedback on previous actions, showing the range of actions available, and making sure the choice to be made is not overwhelming. Other supporting factors include providing clarity on the way in which people are to interact with items, information visualizations, reminders, pop-ups, recommendations, warnings, and personalized messages. Audio, video, animation, simulation, and links to other sites can also contribute to attention and persuasiveness (Fogg, 2002; Sharp et al., 2019).

Websites, apps, or tracking devices may provide users with information pertaining to particular human goals, such as physical exercise, eating, independence, self-direction, achievement, or honor. Feedback may be provided on the impact of everyday activities on the environment, linking to goals of idealism, benevolence, and universalism. Such goals may also be appealed to by apps or systems that allow for sharing or cooperation. Feedback on expenditures can relate to users with the goal of saving, while feedback in car or security systems may support users with the goal of security. The effectiveness of such types of feedback depends on the frequency with which it is provided and the character of visualizations used. In addition to feedback, testimonials may be provided that appeal to users with the goals of power and status. Users with the goal of curiosity may be seduced by promising novel information or insights, while users with the goals of order, social contact, acceptance, face, tradition, or conformity may be appealed to by making conforming statements or actions public to a large audience. Users with the goals of romance, stimulation, and hedonism may be appealed to by sound effects prompting the continuation of types of behavior related to these goals. Ease of use may appeal to users with the goal of tranquility, which may stimulate continuing use. As with social influence in general, once human goals are activated they can be used to influence attitudes, beliefs, and behaviors (Fogg, 2002; Sharp et al., 2019).

Pictures, audio, video, and/or animations with specific content and aesthetics may be used to arouse various emotions, as can artifacts that have been made to appear to have human or animal-like qualities. Websites can arouse excitement, interest, or sexual arousal by promising particular benefits from undertaking certain actions. Physical and inferred personality and identity characteristics of an implementation of technology may activate feelings of love, liking, trust, and joy. Similar feelings can be aroused through messages that address users by name, provide recommendations, ask for feedback, express gratitude, offer praise, or provide joy. Such arousal of emotions as well as inferred emotions such as anger, fear, contempt, and reassurance as seen to be expressed by computers can directly or subsequently be used in attempts to influence behavior (Fogg, 2002; Sharp et al., 2019).

Websites may be more persuasive if they are consistent in design, require simple procedures, and present a clear and coherent organization of items. They may attempt to limit the amount of thinking required by providing just enough information, clear and simple instructions, help functions, and background information (Sharp et al., 2019). Attractiveness of technologies or testimonials by others may activate the halo effect and/or the heuristics of liking and social proof. When users are aware that the information they provide will be publicly accessible and traceable to them, the heuristic of commitment and consistency is activated supporting related types of behavior. Commitment and consistency can also be activated by texts on buttons that need to be clicked. Apps may also ask for reciprocation in return for helpful information that they provided (Fogg, 2002).

Computer systems can be programmed in such a way that they provide advice or information when a user indicates a need for this. The persuasive effect of such advice or information increases with the credibility of the computer systems which depends on the perceived trustworthiness and expertise of such systems. The credibility of computer systems can be enhanced by ease of use, aesthetics, responsiveness, confirming expectations of users, providing personalized content and services, and by demonstrating their capabilities. Openness about the source of the system/website, endorsements by reputable websites, links to external sources, awards, and continued reliable outcomes can support credibility of computer systems as well. In line with Aristotle's ideas on rhetorics, the persuasiveness of computer systems is enhanced by the right timing of relevant suggestions (Fogg, 2002).

Digital media can be mixed, embedded, linked to, tagged, automatically generated, adjusted, and opened up for comments and (automated) replies in an attempt to enhance persuasiveness. Choices of design of digital media may also influence persuasiveness, both in terms of drawing attention and fitting the substance of persuasive messages. For effective persuasion, it is important to keep track of and ensure the availability, content, metadata, and interpretations of archives that are used or linked to. Knowledge and effective use of systems and channels to present persuasive messages, including content management systems, intranet, cloud-based and social media platforms, and communication apps enhance persuasiveness (Eyman, 2015).

Apparent similarities in inferred personality traits and identities of computer systems with their users strengthen the persuasive effects of suggestions made by such systems. Labeling computer systems as if they belong to the same group as a user has a similar effect. A computing system may also present desired identities or role models that may be selected by a user strengthening the persuasive effect of subsequent suggestions by the system. Computers can be programmed to ask for behavioral compliance, as when the demand is made to accept license agreements. Normative pressures by peers may be channeled and activated by computers inciting conformity. Simulator programs provide the possibility of using role playing to change behavior (Fogg, 2002).

Exercises of power over others and empowerment

As mentioned in the introduction to this chapter, understanding how exercises of power over others work empowers by allowing recognition of abusive techniques when these are used. But it also empowers recognition of various ways in which power may be exercised over others in a constructive manner. As we all exercise power continuously, and often over others, this is not a minor issue. Although much research on ways of exercising power over others have been concerned with abuses of power, and it is easy to label exercises of power over others as abusive by definition, in fact, there is no way to avoid exercising power over others. Exposing the ways in which power may be exercised over others hopefully encourages more empowering uses of power.

References

Archer, M. (1996). *Culture and agency: The place of culture in social theory* (rev. ed.). Cambridge: Cambridge University Press.

Arendt, H. (1969). *On violence.* New York: Harcourt, Brace and World.

Aristotle (350 BCa). *The Politics* (B. Jowett, Trans.). Retrieved 22 June 2021, from http://classics.mit.edu/Aristotle/politics.mb.txt.

Aristotle (350 BCb). *Rhetoric* (W.R. Roberts, Trans.). Retrieved 2 December 2020, from http://classics.mit.edu/Aristotle/rhetoric.mb.txt.

Bachrach, P. & Baratz, M. (1963). Decisions and nondecisions: An analytical framework. *American Political Science Review, 69*(3), 900–904. https://doi.org/10.2307/1952568.

Bandura, A. (1986). *Social learning theory.* Englewood Cliffs, NJ: Prentice-Hall.

Beetham, D. (2013). *The legitimation of power* (2nd ed.). Houndmills: Palgrave Macmillan.

Bosch, R. (2016). *Power: A conceptual analysis.* The Hague: Eleven International Publishing.

Bourdieu, P. (1979/1984). *Distinction: A social critique of the judgement of taste* (R. Nice, Trans.). Cambridge, MA: Harvard University Press.

Brey, P. (2008). The technological construction of social power. *Social Epistemology, 22*(1), 71–95.

Chen, Y.-J, Lin, C.-F., & Liu, H.-W. (2018). "Rule of trust": The power and perils of China's social credit megaproject. *Columbia Journal of Asian Law, 32*(1), 1–36. https://doi.org/10.7916/cjal.v32i1.3369.

Cialdini, R.B. (2009). *Influence: Science and practice* (5th ed.). Boston, MA: Pearson Education.

Cicero (84–44 BC/2016). *How to win an argument: An ancient guide to the art of persuasion* (J.M. May, Ed. & Trans.). Princeton, NJ: Princeton University Press.

Clegg, S.R. & Haugaard, M. (Eds.) (2009). *The SAGE handbook of power.* Los Angeles, CA: SAGE.

Clegg, S., Kornberger, M., Pitsis, T.S., & Mount, M. (2019). *Managing & organizations: An introduction to theory and practice* (5th ed.). Los Angeles, CA: SAGE.

Department of Defense (2012). Department of Defense directive number D0DD 3000.09. Washington, DC: U.S. Department of Defense. Retrieved 8 May 2021, from https://www.hsdl.org/?view&did=726163.

Deutsch, M. & Gerard, H.B. (1955). A study of normative and informational social influences upon individual judgment. *Journal of Abnormal and Social Psychology, 51*(3), 629–636. https://doi.org/10.1037/h0046408.

Engelstad, F. (2009). Culture and power. In S.R. Clegg & M. Haugaard (Eds.), *The SAGE handbook of power* (pp. 210–238). Thousand Oaks, CA: SAGE.

Etzioni, A. (1968). *The active society: A theory of societal and political processes.* New York: The Free Press.

Eyman, D. (2015). *Digital rhetoric: Theory, method, practice.* Ann Arbor: University of Michigan Press.

Festinger, L. (1954). A theory of social comparison processes. *Human Relations, 7*, 117–140. https://doi.org/10.1177/001872675400700202.

Fishbein, M. & Ajzen, I. (1975). *Belief, attitude, intention and behavior: An introduction to theory and research.* London: Addison-Wesley.

Fishbein, M. & Ajzen, I. (2010). *Predicting and changing behavior: The reasoned action approach.* New York: Psychology Press.

Flowerdew, J. & Richardson, J.E. (Eds.) (2018). *The Routledge handbook of critical discourse studies.* London: Routledge.

Fogg, B.J. (2002). *Persuasive technology: Using computers to change what we think and do.* Amsterdam: Morgan Kaufmann Publishers.

Foucault, M. (1975/1977). *Discipline and punish: The birth of the prison* (A. Sheridan, Trans.). New York: Random House.

Foucault, M. (1982). Afterword: The subject and power. In H.L. Dreyfus & P. Rabinow (Eds.), *Michel Foucault: Beyond structuralism and hermeneutics* (pp. 208–226). Brighton: The Harvester Press.

Foucault, M. (2003). *Society must be defended: Lectures at the Collège de France 1975–1976.* New York: Picador.

Freeden, M., Sargent, L.T., & Stears, M. (2015). *The Oxford handbook of political ideologies.* Oxford: Oxford University Press.

Goffman, E. (1986). *Frame analysis: An essay on the organization of experience.* Boston, MA: Northeastern University Press.

Gramsci, A. (1971). *Selections from the prison notebooks* (Q. Hoare & G.N. Smith, Trans.). New York: International Publishers.

Greifeneder, R., Jaffé, M.E., Newman, E.J., & Schwarz, N. (2021). What is new and true about fake news? In R. Greifeneder, M.E. Jaffé, E.J. Newman, N., & Schwarz (Eds.), *The psychology of fake news: Accepting, sharing, and correcting misinformation* (pp. 1–8). London: Routledge.

Grimes, R.L. (2013). *The craft of ritual studies.* Oxford: Oxford University Press.

Hall, E. (2018). *Aristotle's way: How ancient wisdom can change your life.* London: Vintage.

Handelman, D. (1990). *Models and mirrors: Towards an anthropology of public events.* New York: Berghahn Books.

Haslam, S.A., Reicher, S.D., & Platow, M.J. (2011). *The New psychology of leadership: Identity, influence and power.* New York: Psychology Press.

Haugaard, M. & Clegg, S.R. (2009). Introduction: Why power is the central concept of the social sciences. In S.R. Clegg & M. Haugaard (Eds.), *The SAGE handbook of power* (pp. 1–24). Thousand Oaks, CA: SAGE.

Heywood, A. (2017). *Political ideologies: An introduction* (6th ed.). London: Palgrave.

Hobbes, T. (1651/1996). *Leviathan.* Oxford: Oxford University Press.

Kahneman, D. (2011). *Thinking fast and slow.* New York: Farrar, Straus and Giroux.

Kraus, J. (2015). *Rhetoric in European culture and beyond.* Prague: Karolinum Press.

Krishnan, A. (2009). *Killer robots: Legality and ethicality of autonomous weapons.* Burlington, VT: Ashgate.

Latour, B. (2005). *Reassembling the social: An introduction to actor-network theory.* Oxford: Oxford University Press.

Lenski, G. (1966). *Power and privilege: A theory of social stratification.* New York: McGraw-Hill.

Letwin, W.L. (1954). The English common law concerning monopolies. *The University of Chicago Law Review, 21*(3), 355–385.

Lukes, S. (1995). Power. Paper presented at the European University Institute, Florence, Italy.

Machiavelli, N. (1521/2003). *Art of war* (C. Lynch, Ed. & Trans.). Chicago, IL: University of Chicago Press.

Machiavelli, N. (1532/2009). *The prince* (T. Parks, Trans.). London: Penguin Books.

Mannheim, K. (1929/1936). *Ideology and utopia: An introduction to the sociology of knowledge* (L. Wirth & E. Shils, Trans.). London: Routledge & Kegan Paul.

McBrayer, J.P. (2021). *Beyond fake news: Finding the truth in a world of misinformation.* London: Routledge.

Montesquieu (1748/1989). *The spirit of the laws* (A.M. Cohler, B.C. Miller, & H.S. Stone, Eds.). Cambridge: Cambridge University Press.

Morgan, G. (1986). *Images of organization.* Thousand Oaks, CA: SAGE.

Parsons, T. (1963). On the concept of political power. *Political Studies Review, 4*(2), 124–135.

Pasquale, F. (2020). *New laws of robotics: Defending human expertise in the age of AI.* Cambridge, MA: The Belknap Press of Harvard University Press.

Paulus, P.B. (Ed.) (1989). *Psychology of group influence* (2nd ed.). Hillsdale, NJ: Lawrence Erlbaum Associates.

Perry, S. & Roda, C. (2017). *Human rights and digital technology: Digital tightrope.* London: Palgrave Macmillan.

Petty, R.E. & Briñol, P. (2010). Attitude change. In R.F. Baumeister & E.J. Finkel (Eds.), *Advanced social psychology: The state of the science* (pp. 217–259). Oxford: Oxford University Press.

Poggi, G. (2001). *Forms of power*. Cambridge: Polity.

Powell, W.W. (1991). Expanding the scope of institutional analysis. In W.W. Powell & P.J. DiMaggio (Eds.), *The new institutionalism in organizational analysis* (pp. 183–203). Chicago, IL: The University of Chicago Press.

Rae, G. & Ingala, E. (Eds.) (2018). *The meanings of violence: From critical theory to biopolitics*. New York: Routledge.

Ramage, J.D., Bean, J.C., & Johnson, J. (2015). *Writing arguments: A rhetoric with readings* (Concise 7th ed.). Boston, MA: Pearson.

Russell, B. (1938). *Power: A new social analysis*. London: Allen and Unwin.

Ryan, K. (2009). Power and exclusion. In S.R. Clegg & M. Haugaard (Eds.), *The SAGE handbook of power* (pp. 348–366). Thousand Oaks, CA: SAGE.

Sayer, A. (2012). Power, causality and normativity: A critical realist critique of Foucault. *Journal of Political Power, 5*(2), 179–194. https://doi.org/10.1080/21583 79X.2012.698898.

Scott, J. (2001). *Power*. Cambridge: Polity.

Segal, R.A. (2015). *Myth: A very short introduction*. Oxford: Oxford University Press.

Sewell, G. (2021). *Surveillance: A key idea for business and society*. London: Routledge.

Sharp, H., Rogers, Y., & Preece, J. (2019). *Interaction design: Beyond human computer interaction* (5th ed.). Indianapolis, IN: Wiley.

Skinner, Q. (1988). Language and social change. In J. Tully (Ed.), *Meaning and context: Quentin skinner and his critics* (pp. 119–132). Cambridge: Polity Press.

Stephenson, B. (2015). *Ritual: A very short introduction*. Oxford: Oxford University Press.

Sun, T. (6th cent. BC/1971). *The art of war* (S.B. Griffith, Trans.). Oxford: Oxford University Press.

Symantec (2019). *ISTR: Internet security threat report. Volume 24.* Retreived 26 January 2021, from https://docs.broadcom.com/doc/istr-24-2019-en.

Torfing, J. (2009). Power and discourse: Towards an anti-foundationalist concept of power. In S.R. Clegg & M. Haugaard (Eds.), *The SAGE handbook of power* (pp. 108–124). Thousand Oaks, CA: SAGE.

Toulmin, S. (2003). *The uses of arguments* (updated ed.). Cambridge: Cambridge University Press.

Tully, J. (Ed.) (1988). *Meaning and context: Quentin skinner and his critics*. Cambridge: Polity Press.

Turner, V. (1967). *The forest of symbols: Aspects of Ndembu ritual*. Ithaca, NY: Cornell University Press.

Van Gennep, A. (1908/1960). *The rites of passage* (M.B. Vizedom & G.L. Caffee, Trans.). Chicago, IL: The University of Chicago Press.

Von Clausewitz, C. (1832/1989). *On war* (M. Howard & P. Paret, Eds. & Trans.). Princeton, NJ: Princeton University Press.

Winner, L. (1980). Do artifacts have politics? *Daedalus, 109*(1), 121–136.

Yan, W.Q. (2019). *Introduction to intelligent surveillance: Surveillance data capture, transmission, and analytics* (3rd ed.). Cham: Springer.

Zimbardo, P.G. & Leippe, M.R. (1991). *The psychology of attitude change and social influence*. New York: McGraw-Hill.

Zuboff, S. (1988). *In the age of the smart machine: The future of work and power*. New York: Basic Books.

5

STRATEGY

Based on structures of power and individual power, power can be exercised. The way in which this is done can be interpreted to follow a more or less explicit strategy. Seen this way, strategy constitutes a process which may be preceded by or include a more or less conscious planning of steps. In line with this idea, the term 'strategy' will here be used to refer to the processual development of plans for and/or the undertaking of courses of action to employ means to achieve goals. The idea of strategy as a process leaves room for combining the idea of strategy as a planning process with that of strategy as strategic patterns of action (Mintzberg & Waters, 1985). In other words, to some extent strategy can be seen as developed consciously and more or less in advance of its implementation, but to some extent it may be the outcome of an interpretation of actual patterns of action regarding a strategic issue which may include ongoing learning processes (Andersen, 2013).

Whether strategy is conceived as planning or as embodied in patterns of action, it can be seen to consist of a number of phases which may or may not be explicit during the strategy process. These phases, which may occur iteratively and in an intermingled fashion, include strategic assessment, the determination of strategic goals, the development of strategic approaches, the implementation of strategic courses of action, and strategic interactions. Knowing about strategy is highly empowering, because it supports the development of strategies as well as potential recognition of the strategies of others.

Strategic assessment

Sun's (6th cent. BC/1971) classical analysis of military strategy in *The Art of War* starts with an emphasis on the importance of assessment. According to Sun, five factors need to be assessed: the moral influence of leaders over their people

DOI: 10.4324/9781003034100-6

to establish a shared sense of purpose; the weather; the terrain; command of the leadership as based on wisdom, sincerity, humanity, courage, and strictness; and 'doctrine', consisting of organization, control, the assignment of appropriate ranks, regulation of supply, and adequate provision. These factors are to be assessed, respectively, by looking at the ability of leaders, the way in which the weather and the terrain provide advantages, the extent to which regulations and instructions are carried out, the strength of troops in terms of training, and the extent to which rewards and punishments are administered in an enlightened fashion. It is clear from Sun's writings that such assessments need to be performed of supporting factors as well as opposing ones. In order to do the latter, Sun suggests the use of provocations and spies. Translated into contemporary strategic terms, Sun's prescriptions entail an assessment of the ability of leaders to achieve a shared sense of purpose, an analysis of relevant situations and fields (i.e., transsituational networks of relations between positions in structures of power), an evaluation of the effectiveness of direction in terms of wisdom, sincerity, humanity, courage, and strictness, and an assessment of the quality of organization, control, training, and incentive systems.

In another military classic, *On War*, Von Clausewitz (1832/1989) also argued for the importance of assessment. According to Von Clausewitz, power consists of the total means available, which are to be measured, and strength of will, which is to be gauged approximately. Available resources include the fighting forces, the country with its physical features and population, and allies. Essential is the existence of what Von Clausewitz calls 'military genius': mental powers that include courage, intelligence, determination, presence of mind, energy, firmness, staunchness, endurance, emotional stability, strength of character, a sense of locality, and combat experience. According to Von Clausewitz, a leader should be politically savvy, recognize other leaders, understand the people that are to be commanded, have the ability to form sound judgments, and be knowledgeable of tactical principles, rules, and routines. An assessment of the situation at hand is also considered indispensable. This includes looking at the terrain, the time of day, the weather, and other relevant situational facts and their causes.

Contemporary military views on strategic assessment argue for a comprehensive approach. For both sides of a potential conflict, an attempt should be made to measure potentially relevant objectives, ways to achieve them, available resources, existing risks, and scenarios. This is to be done in an iterative process, where each new piece of information requires a reconsideration of assessments (Yarger, 2012). The operational environment is to be analyzed according to the acronym PMESII-PT: Political, Military, Economic, Social, Infrastructure, Information, Physical terrain, and Time. This implies looking at political conditions, military capabilities, economic production, distribution, and consumption, and cultural, religious, and ethnic compositions. It also implies analyzing the basic infrastructural facilities, services, and installations, geography and man-made physical structures, the way in which information is collected, processed, disseminated, and acted upon, and the timing and duration of activities, events, and conditions (Headquarters Department of the Army, 2014).

In the field of business, approaches have been developed to perform similar comprehensive strategic assessments. Such assessments may focus on strategically relevant resources, competences, capabilities, or available knowledge and technologies. They may also consider management practices and policies, aspects of organization and culture, characteristics of industries, factors at a macro-level, and/or future growth opportunities. The value, expenses on, and costs of existing and required financial and nonfinancial resources can be assessed using accounting tools such as balance sheets, income statements, financial ratios, cash flows, balanced scorecards, cost-volume-profit analyses, cost systems, customer profitability analysis, and budgets (Atkinson et al., 2012; Andersen, 2013; Desai, 2019). Core competences may be identified based on the access they provide to various markets, the contribution they make to perceived customer benefits, and the difficulty with which they can be imitated by others. The combined functioning of relevant resources, competences, capabilities, available knowledge and technologies, products and product quality, management practices and policies, and aspects of organization and culture can be assessed using value chain analysis, benchmarks, historical analyses, business model analyses, organizational typologies, and models such as McKinsey 7S and VRIO. Such analyses may be performed for supporting as well as opposing businesses (Prahalad & Hamel, 1990; Andersen, 2013; Grant, 2018; Pidun, 2019).

Characteristics of relevant industries may be assessed by means of the elaborate structural analysis suggested by Porter (1980/1998). Porter's analysis implies looking at a multitude of aspects relevant to a particular industry related to five overarching factors: the threat of new entrants, rivalry among competitors, the threat of substitute products or services, the bargaining power of buyers, and the bargaining power of suppliers. The threat of new entrants is to be evaluated by assessing the following aspects:

- existing economies of scale
- existing product differentiation
- capital required for entry
- customer costs for switching suppliers
- the need of access to distribution channels
- cost advantages, resources, and commitments of competitors
- government policies
- the growth rate of the industry

The second factor, rivalry among existing competitors, is to be assessed by looking at:

- the number, size, and characteristics of competitors
- the growth rate of the industry

- fixed and storage costs
- product differentiation
- switching costs
- required capacity increments
- exit barriers

The third factor, the threat posed by substitute products or services, can be assessed by estimating:

- the price-performance alternative offered by substitute products or services
- the financial situation of their providers

The bargaining power of buyers, the fourth factor, should be estimated by looking at:

- the portion of sales of particular buyers
- the fraction of their overall expenses constituted by their purchases
- the standardization of the products or services
- the buyers' switching costs
- the buyers' profit levels
- the potential of buyers for backward integration
- the relevance of the quality of the product or service
- the information possessed by the buyers.

The final factor, the bargaining power of suppliers, can be gauged by considering the following aspects:

- the number of suppliers and buyers in the industry
- existing substitute products
- the relevance of the industry to the suppliers
- the relevance of the product or service to the buyers
- existing differentiation of the products or services
- switching costs for the buyers
- the potential for forward integration
- the degree of organization and potential for expansion of required types of labor

Porter's elaborate list of factors to be assessed gives a good indication of what comprehensive assessment may entail, but his list has been extended even further with the inclusion of assessments of firms that offer complementary goods and services and that may introduce a level of inter-firm cooperation. A level of cooperation may also exist with suppliers and customers, which implies the existence of industrial clusters that may be analyzed. The phase of the industry, such as growth, maturity, or innovation, may also be taken into account, as may changes in business models describing new ways of doing business, new products, and changes in the uses of technology. A stakeholder analysis can be performed by identifying and analyzing all groups that have an interest in, or are of interest to, a firm. This may include customers, financiers, unions, local communities, competitors, government agencies, suppliers, special interest groups, and the media (Freeman et al., 2010; Andersen, 2013).

Factors at a macro-level can be analyzed using the acronym PEST, which refers to Political, Economic, Social, and Technological factors. This implies assessing political issues such as government policies, elections, trade negotiations, and social unrest; economic conditions such as production and demand, prices, and financial figures and trends; social developments such as demographics, prevailing norms and beliefs, networks of social relationships, and educational levels; and technological developments, such as production technologies and scientific developments. The acronym has at times be extended to PESTLE to include analyzing legal conditions such as existing legislation, jurisprudence, and law enforcement, and environmental issues, such as pollution, climate developments, and sustainability. An assessment can be made of how the factors captured by the PESTLE acronym impact on the characteristics of relevant industries (Andersen, 2013; Grant, 2018).

The various ways to perform internal and external strategic assessments in business may be combined. In a SWOT analysis, internal and external assessments are brought together in order to analyze internal strengths and weaknesses and external opportunities and threats. Scenarios can be developed based on assessments concerning the development and relations between factors that are considered key (Andersen, 2013).

In government too, assessments may be performed to support public strategies. Internal strengths and weaknesses may be assessed, as well as external threats and opportunities. This may be done for various policy fields, whether these are concerned with economic, social, health, or educational issues. Inventarisations can be made of needs and capabilities of stakeholders, constituencies, and society at large. National accounts and various types of national statistics can be helpful in such assessments as can regulation that coerces organizations and citizens to provide various types of information such as financial accounts and income statements. To assess general economic competitiveness, Porter (1990) proposed using the 'diamond' framework which suggests analyzing factor/resource conditions, demand conditions, the existence of related and supporting industries, and strategies, structures, and rivalry of firms. Analytical typologies may also be used to assess national economic systems, looking at issues such as corporate governance, inter-firm relations, industrial relations, and educational systems (Hall & Soskice, 2001; Johanson, 2019).

In a general sense, comprehensive assessment implies analyzing power structures, existing individual and collective powers, exercises of power, and strategies and the interactions that result from them in sufficient detail. This provides an assessment of abilities, how these have led to interactions, and how they could lead to interactions in the future. On the basis of this, preparations can be made, and sources and means of power, and ways of exercising power can be selected (Sun, 6th cent. BC/1971; Machiavelli, 1532/2009; Bosch, 2016).

The impact of ICT on strategic assessment

Over the past decades, the possibility for comprehensive assessment has increased significantly due to technological developments, particularly in ICT. ICT systems not only allow for extensive and affordable storage and efficient processing and analysis of information, they also allow for the active collection of information through the internet and all the machines and objects that are connected to it. Storage capacities have increased immensely as have processing capabilities, including those supported by data science and AI applications.

Data that might be useful for assessment is everywhere. It depends on the type of assessment to be performed what kind of data may be collected. Relevant data may be found both on- and offline in various texts, images, movies, and audio files, semi-structured forms such as HTML, XML, JSON, CSV, and server logs, databases, and archives. Such data may be gathered from libraries, the front and backends of media platforms, and web pages, the cloud, the internet of things, and customized databases and archives. Data may also be actively collected by means of direct observations, interviews, surveys, measuring, recording, or through devices linked to the internet by means of logging, tracking, hacking, or interactive ('smart') applications, devices, and infrastructures. Information systems may collect, record, store, and process data that can be used in assessments. To be able to process such data using ICT applications, the data needs to be extracted, formatted, organized, stored, and analyzed. For this, techniques such as automatic coding, natural language processing, data mining, statistical analyses and models, deep learning and other AI techniques, and visualizations can be used. The outcome of such analyses may consist of descriptions, predictions, and/or prescriptions that can be used in assessments (Romney & Steinbart, 2018; Harari, 2019; Berthold et al., 2020; Burdon, 2020; Gupta et al., 2020).

Apart from providing support in strategic assessment, ICT systems themselves may also be assessed. This may imply an assessment of ICT resources in terms of hardware, software, and ICT operators, strategic policies in the cyber field, possibilities for and conditions of cyber attack and defense, and responsibility attribution possibilities. It also implies analyzing the legal, economic, and social contexts of ICT capabilities, as well as their industrial applications. To assess such factors for (potential) adversaries, cyber exploitation can be used, which includes penetrating ICT networks of (potential) adversaries. This way, strengths and weaknesses may be identified, as well as the setup of systems, their components, and the way they function. Another way to find out about such aspects of ICT systems is by using spies (Brantly, 2016).

The determination of goals

After at least some more or less conscious assessment, strategic goals can be distinguished related to such assessment. When this is done consciously and formally in an organization, a mission statement may be developed to indicate a long-term overall direction. This may consist of a vision which presents a purpose for which an organization exists, aspirations and goals to be achieved, a set of values, and guidelines for behavior. The development and interpretation of such a mission, vision, goals, values, and behavioral guidelines may occur in a top-down and/or bottom-up fashion. When a top-down approach is taken, a cascading approach can be used, where overarching goals are decided upon first, after which goals are decided upon with a more limited scope. In practice, the determination of goals often, at least to some extent, follows a bottom-up process. This may go so far as resulting in 'open strategy', a process in which a wide range of people is included into the overall strategy process. When strategy is seen as embodied in actual practices, strategic goals can also be interpreted after the fact in terms of strategic effects of actual patterns of behavior (Ansoff, 1965; Mintzberg & Waters, 1985; Andersen, 2013; Seidl et al., 2019).

Which goals are pursued depends on the type of entity. Goals that may be pursued by individuals were discussed in Chapter 3. For organizations, goals may range from victory in battle or successful defense for military organizations, to value creation for stakeholders, competitiveness, survival, growth, technological leadership and/or environmental, social, and governance goals for businesses, and policy and social goals for governments and non-governmental organizations. Such overarching goals are translated into or may interpretively result from a manifold of specific goals. In this process, the SMART method can be used, which aims at making goals specific, measurable, assignable, realistic, and time-related so as to enhance their effectiveness (Porter, 1980/1998; Bjerke & Renger, 2017; Grant, 2018; Pidun, 2019).

The determination of goals can lead to a more extensive or revised assessment, which, in its turn, may lead to changes in goals, and so on, iteratively. Evaluations based on performance indicators may also lead to changes in formally pursued goals. More or less unexpected internal or external developments may lead to reassessments and revisions in and changes of goals, as may the outcomes of strategic planning processes (Andersen, 2013; Grant, 2018; Pidun, 2019).

Developments in ICT have provided a bottom-up influence on the determination of goals by allowing the inclusion of a wide range of people in the process. Suggestions relevant to the determination of goals can be made and obtained efficiently through email, internal communication platforms, social media platforms, blogs, and video meetings. Surveys and interviews can be administered easily and effectively (Morton et al., 2019). The determination of goals can also be supported by data science and AI applications that provide analyses and suggestions in the form of scenarios and predictions (Corea, 2019; Shah, 2020).

Strategic approaches

When some assessment has been performed and a certain direction of intention has been chosen – whether or not explicitly supported by strategic goals – strategic approaches may be more or less consciously selected. In Sun's (6th cent. BC/1971, p. 66) words, this implies the intent to "act expediently in accordance with what is advantageous and so control the balance". In order to do so, a number of specific exercises of power can be combined, potentially into an overall strategic plan (Andersen, 2013).

From Sun's (6th cent. BC/1971) *The Art of War,* an overall strategic approach can be reconstructed that contains a number of elements. A first element is the extensive use of deception. Attempts can be made to hide capabilities, activities, assessments, and plans so as to make it seem these do not exist. Locations can be concealed, disorderliness can be feigned, applied strategies can be alternated, and opponents can be made to believe that their strategies work. Opponents may also be emotionally deceived by angering or tiring them or by stimulating their arrogance. When such deception is used, inducements can be used to lure opponents into situations where they may be attacked. At the same time, attempts at deception by opponents should be warded off. Other elements of Sun's strategy include an adequate preparation of resources, the appropriation of resources from opponents, and the use of divide and conquer. According to Sun, it is best to win without fighting, and if conflicts are necessary, they should not be protracted. To achieve this, strength should be avoided while weakness should be attacked. By means of skillful positioning, a position may be attained from which it is clear that victory can be achieved so that actual conflict becomes unnecessary. Normal forces may be kept separate from extraordinary forces, so that the latter may be used to attain swift victories. Opponents can be weakened by wearing them out, disheartening them, starving them, or inducing them into actions they actually do not wish to perform. Diversions can be used to slow them down. Opponents that have lost should be left a possibility to survive so that unnecessary further conflict can be avoided. Which specific strategic elements are to be used depends on the situation: for instance, preparing resources is of major importance in situations of defense, whereas appropriation of resources from opponents is important in situations of offense.

Von Clausewitz (1832/1989) proposed a strategy with a different focus. In his view, strategy should primarily be concerned with the annihilation of the enemy's forces. This should be attained by means of a decisive 'great battle'. The strategy to be used up to and including the great battle should be formulated into a plan which specifies the series of actions to pursue, while remaining flexible in light of the situation in which the strategy is applied. Rather similar to Sun's ideas, strategic elements to be used include the preparation of forces, the building of alliances, the disruption of alliances of opponents, the appropriation of the opponents' resources, the use of surprise and trickery, the concentration of forces in time and space, maintaining a strategic reserve, and an economic management of forces. During conflict, attention should be paid to what Von Clausewitz called the 'culminating point of attack'. At that point, forces have been weakened to such an extent that further attacks should be halted (Bosch, 2016).

Contemporary military approaches categorize strategies in a number of ways. First, strategies may be declaratory (what they are claimed to be), actual (what they are in practice), and ideal (what they would ideally be). Second, strategies may be sequential, simultaneous, or cumulative. They may consist of attrition (gradual destruction), exhaustion (eroding the will and resources of opponents), or annihilation (complete destruction). Strategies can be based on deterrence, compellence, or reassurance. They can be relevant to different levels of operations, ranging from grand or national strategies to campaign or operational strategies. An overall iterative military strategy may include processes of assessment, goal determination, strategy development, preparation of resources, plan development, and implementation. Components of strategy can include the use of secrecy, deception, and confusion, avoiding strength and attacking weakness, undertaking great battles, defensive actions, and various combinations of more or less tactical uses of force (Bosch, 2016; Bartholomees, 2012; Freedman, 2013).

For business units, Porter (1980/1998) distinguished three generic strategies. In a strategy aimed at cost leadership, strategic activities include efficient scale production, cost reduction, tight cost and overhead control, avoidance of marginal customers, and cost minimization in support function activities. Efficient scale production may require large investments in equipment and the design of products that are closely related, easy to produce, and that serve large customer groups. A generic strategy of differentiation of products or services entails design and branding activities, the development of specific technologies or features in products, or providing differentiating customer services. The third generic strategy consists of a focus on particular buyers, product line segments, or geographic markets. In this strategy, activities are aimed specifically at meeting the needs arising from the focus that is taken.

Corporate strategy is concerned with the constitution of a firm's portfolio of business units. Here, strategies may aim at unrelated diversification, horizontal coordination, or vertical integration. For unrelated diversification, business units that offer unrelated products or services are formed into conglomerates with the aim to achieve risk reduction and synergy among shared functions. Horizontal coordination implies the coordination of goals and strategies of related business units. This allows for the sharing of various components of the value chain, such as financing, production, and marketing activities as well as different types of knowledge. Vertical integration refers to inclusion of activities performed by suppliers or buyers. Such a strategy may reduce costs and risks and enhance internal coordination (Porter, 1985, 1980/1998).

A final type of strategy suggested by Porter (2008) is that of corporate location in light of the existence of industrial clusters – geographic concentrations of interconnected companies and institutions that compete but also cooperate. Corporate location inside such a cluster may provide access to required infrastructure, suppliers, maintenance capabilities, competences, knowledge, and opportunities for innovation. This contrasts with a strategy of locating business activities in areas with low wage and commodity costs.

A number of additional business and corporate strategies have been distinguished. A well-known business strategy is that of tacit collusion, when different businesses in an industry cooperate to reduce competition without explicitly agreeing to do so. Additional corporate strategies include such activities as the strategic location of production in light of the value chain, outsourcing, offshoring, downsizing, the formation of strategic alliances, and the use of mergers and acquisitions (Grant, 2018; Barney & Hesterly, 2019).

Focusing on the nature of strategies, Mintzberg and Waters (1985) distinguished eight types. In the type of strategies that are planned, strategic plans exist that indicate intentions, controls, and deliberate strategic elements. When strategies are entrepreneurial, intentions only exist in the mind of an entrepreneur, control is personal, and strategies may be deliberate or they may emerge from actual actions. Ideological types of strategies are characterized by a collective vision based on shared beliefs, and supported by indoctrination, socialization, and deliberate strategic elements. With an umbrella strategy, strategic boundaries or targets are defined by leadership, but actors may respond autonomously and in response to the environment, thereby making strategic elements partly deliberate and partly emergent. In process strategies, supportive processes are controlled while strategic goals and elements arise out of actions. Unconnected strategies exist where strategies originate in separate enclaves. Consensus strategies refer to strategies that arise out of mutual adjustment in various activities. And finally, imposed strategies refer to strategies that result from environmental pressures dictating activities.

On a more detailed level, business strategies may contain various components. A first component is constituted by activities addressing gaps in capabilities. Training programs and R&D projects may be started to attain needed competences. Ways to handle existing internal resistances and cultural barriers may be considered as well. Timetables with key performance indicators can be drawn up to coordinate activities and monitor progress. Contingency plans can be drawn up to deal with potential calamities, and flexibility can be built into strategic plans to handle unexpected developments (Andersen, 2013). Quality improvement processes, the nature of advertisements, and offensive and defensive market activities can all be components of an overall strategy. Strategic components found in military strategies, such as the use of deception, surprise, escalation, envelopment, and attrition may also be part of business strategies (Grant, 2018; Barney & Hesterly, 2019).

For government, Johanson (2019) distinguishes between macro strategies at the national level and micro strategies of public agencies. Where the prime component of macro strategies consists of regulation of various kinds, on a micro level, public strategies such as networking are often contingent on the macro level governmental strategies that affect the environment of the agencies. On both levels, strategies can include the use of policies, particular organizational structures, rules of thumb for performance measurement, and the management of external interactions. In the context of international relations, Nye (2004) argues for a governmental strategy that combines 'hard power' social control techniques such as force and coercion with that of 'soft power' legitimation and social influence techniques such as persuasion.

Strategies concerned with social power sometimes include calls to the use of violence. Such use of violence may not only destroy existing structures of power, it may also instill fear among those (potentially) subject to it which may support the attainment or maintenance of social power (Machiavelli, 1519/1981; Malesevic, 2009). In stark contrast to this stands Sharp's (2013) strategy of nonviolent struggle. According to Sharp, possibilities for positions and exercises of power by a ruling party always depend on the consent of the ruled. This implies that when such consent is withdrawn, positions of power can be destroyed and exercises of power can be halted. Strategic nonviolent action can consist of protest and persuasion that can be expressed in formal statements, public communications, symbolic acts, pressures on individual functionaries, use of the arts, processions, honoring martyrs, public assemblies, and withdrawals and renunciations. Another form of strategic nonviolent action is noncooperation, which may take the form of ostracism, withdrawals from institutions, economic relationships, customs, events, work, daily life, homes, or the country, or moving to a place that is considered sacred. Economic boycotts or strikes may be pursued, authorities may be rejected, or participation in governmental processes may be halted. Compliance may be delayed in one way or another or it may be deliberately distorted. When a strategy of nonviolent intervention is chosen, nonviolent psychological or physical interventions may be pursued, such as harassment or occupations. Or social, economic, or political interventions may be undertaken, including such processes as setting up alternative communication systems, developing alternative markets, or demonstrating civil disobedience.

According to Olsen's (1970) power and conflict approach, a strategy to attain social power consists of five stages. The first stage consists of organization to bring resources together. This is to be followed by a process of power exertion in which pressure is put on functionaries in critical positions by creating tensions and potential conflicts. During the third stage of confrontation, negotiation and bargaining processes are to occur in order to reach compromises. The fourth stage of social change begins when the agreements are implemented by the key functionaries in the form of policies or legislation. In the final stage, attitude change in society may be achieved in the desired direction (Bosch, 2016). More recent approaches to the attainment of social power have emphasized the importance of media strategies aimed at achieving visibility and participation in the public debate (Meikle, 2018).

In a general sense, strategies consist of combinations of various ways of exercising power. These may take the form of activating individual or collective agency to constructive uses of power, but they may also include various ways of exercising power over others by means of various social control, legitimation, and social influence techniques. Attempts may be made to strengthen structures of power by increasing dependencies on which they rest or to undermine them by reducing such dependencies.

Strategic approaches with ICT

With the expanding global interconnectedness of devices through ICT has come an interest in strategic approaches oriented at and working through ICT systems. In the military field, such approaches are embodied in strategic cyber operations which may be general, defensive, or offensive. General strategies include the more or less conscious use of digital deception and disinformation as well as espionage. They also include the use of general military operations such as organization, training, and equipment provision, intelligence dissemination, logistical support, global command and control, strategic collaborations, and the stimulation of technological innovation. Strategic defensive cyber operations may include such practices as physically defending power supplies and equipment, closing down communication links between networks, removing devices from networks, systems maintenance, the use of encryption, and strengthening resistances to various types of hacking. Offensive strategies include attack planning, the offensive use of robots, IoT devices, Denial of Service attacks, hacking, network mapping, digital forensics, and physical attacks on ICT capabilities of opponents to attain strategic goals (Brantly, 2016).

Elements of military ICT oriented strategies may be applied in business, although legal impediments exist that restrict many such applications. In the field of business, ICT strategies tend rather to be concerned with value-oriented data analytical techniques, ranging from the collection of data, to processes of description, prediction, and prescription. The alignment of such processes with strategic goals can be analyzed by means of such techniques as portfolio analysis, optimization, and simulation modeling. In portfolio analysis, different opportunities offered by applications of data analytical techniques are drawn up, after which they may be prioritized through consensus formation, scoring models, or discounted cash flow analyses. Optimization methods aim to determine optimal combinations of decision variables (such as price levels or production quantities) to achieve strategic goals subject to assessed restraints (such as production capacities) and interpreted relations between the decision variables, goals, and restraints. These methods may use various algorithms to suggest possibilities for the decision variables. Simulation models draw up various scenarios that allow an interpretation of what choices between strategic approaches may entail (Williams, 2016; Prevos, 2019; Albright & Winston, 2020).

Government strategic approaches with ICT may be concerned with governance and regulation as well as public service delivery, private sector support, and international cooperation. In governance strategies, choices may be made which and how much data to collect on citizens, companies, and foreign governments, how to analyze such data, and what to do with the findings. Regulatory strategies may be concerned with choices of regulation of (parts of) the internet in terms of authorities of government and private parties, access and availability (including censorship and moderation), data security, and privacy protection. Public service strategies are concerned with ways to provide public services through websites, social media, and by means of ICT applications. This may also include strategies aimed at training government personnel, and empowering citizens by offering access channels to public decision making and providing transparency. Private sector support strategies may include the pursue of public-private partnerships, and the support of innovations in ICT and necessary infrastructures. Strategies of international cooperation may provide support in the development of ICT capabilities and the attainment of effective regulation (Anderson et al., 2015).

Strategies aimed at attaining social power may involve ICT through the strategic use of digitized media. Such use may include the revealing of personal information about individuals or organizations or disclosure of classified documents and data on websites and social media platforms, and attempts at making communications and frames go viral on the internet through massive posting and sharing. It may also include attempts at social movement organization and collective identity formation, and protest tactics, such as flash mobs, hacktivism, bulk emailing, and Distributed Denial of Service (DDoS) attacks. Other strategic elements may include political strategies including the promotion of ideologies, the provision of open source software and creative common licenses, the use of cryptography and blockchain, design activism oriented at opposing algorithmic exploitation, biases, and control, and data activism, which includes the use of encryption, anti-tracking software, the modification of data, and the exploitation of algorithms to enhance visibility and impact (Lievrouw, 2018; Meikle, 2018; Clegg et al., 2019).

The implementation of strategic courses of action

Implementation of strategic courses of action can be based on preconfigured strategic plans, but it can also consist of performing actions with strategic significance that were not planned in advance. Often, a process of implementation will combine a more or less explicit notion of a strategic plan with unplanned *ad hoc* acting with strategic relevance. This means that during implementation, deliberate strategy tends to become mixed with what has been called 'emergent strategy' – the decisions that emerge from the processes in which strategies are interpreted and adapted to the circumstances (Mintzberg & Waters, 1985).

To the extent that strategy is deliberate, implementation entails the communication of strategic objectives and plans, the setting up of projects and organizational units, the drawing up and communication of concrete action plans and budgets, the stimulation, organization, and control of corresponding actions by designated actors, and the drawing up of time plans and performance measures. If a strategy is flexible, ongoing performance evaluations and changes in the environment may lead to a switch in or planned adjustment of scenarios that still form part of the deliberate strategy. At the same time, performed strategically relevant decisions or actions that are not part of the deliberate strategy may become included as emergent elements. This can be facilitated by a flexible attitude in which deliberate strategy is based on general long-term goals while an overly specific planning of details is avoided. Progress toward strategic goals may be evaluated in regular meetings, where potential adaptations can be discussed and selected. This may lead to adjustments to overall strategies followed by a new process of implementation (Andersen, 2013; Grant, 2018).

Implementation of strategy also entails the concrete planning, activation, and use of ICT systems. In a general sense, this may refer to the use of ICT systems for administrative purposes, communication, or data collection and processing. In the military case, it may include the activation of various types of cyber weapons whether for defensive or offensive purposes (Lin & Zegart, 2019). In the business case, it may entail the use of various types of communication platforms ranging from websites to intranet or cloud-based communication systems, production systems based on IT, robotics, and/or cloud-based solutions, and data storage and analysis systems (Morton et al., 2019; Prevos, 2019). For government, it may imply activating ICT-based communication, service delivery, governance, and empowerment systems (Anderson et al., 2015). And in the case of strategies aimed at social power, it may include the activation of social media strategies (Meikle, 2018).

Strategic interactions

Implementations of strategies, whether these are planned or result from actions with strategic implications, always occur in situations that form part of specific fields – particular areas of social life constituted by networks of relations between positions in structures of power. Fields include such social entities as the state, policy domains, the economy, firms, markets, the media, classes, but also lower-level entities such as organizational units, neighborhoods, families, and so on. Fields constitute the 'arenas' in which situational interactions occur. In situations and fields, various types of interactions may take place when actions by different actors occur in similar places at similar times. When actions by others do not interfere with strategic actions, they are not important to the implementation of strategies. When actions by others do interfere with strategic actions, they are relevant to implementation. When such actions by others are oriented at similar strategic goals, they imply a situation of strategic interaction (Goffman, 1961; Bourdieu & Wacquant, 1992; Fligstein & McAdam, 2012).

Interactions may occur in several forms. Two important forms are coordination and cooperation. Coordination implies the harmonization of actions, movements, or conditions, while cooperation refers to working together with others. These types of interactions constitute forms of collective power which will be discussed in the next chapter. A third form of interaction is that of interactive communication, a process in which information is exchanged through linguistic symbols, signs, or behavior. According to the theory of coordinated management of meaning, interactive communication starts with a process of assigning meaning to the communicative situation and information provided by others in that situation. This is followed by a communicative response, which may entail a process of interpersonal accommodation, adaptation, and approachment or, alternatively, one of resistance and divergence. This may be followed by a response by others, which may again be responded to, and so on. In this process, the social context provides frames and rules that influence interpretations and responses. The interactive communication process is also affected by salient structures of power, individual and collective power, exercises of power, and strategies. If interactive communication is successful, it results in stories describing what has been communicated that may or may not be shared by participants to the process. If the stories are shared, some sort of mutual understanding has been reached. But messages may be unclear, leading to differences in stories and misunderstandings. In light of the importance of communication for exercises of power described in the previous chapter, the outcomes of interactive communication can have significant effects on structures of power (Bosch, 2016; Littlejohn et al., 2017).

A fourth form of interaction is imitation. In interaction, imitation consists of more or less successful attempts at the repetition of actions performed by others participating in the interaction. Such imitation may be based on habits, norms, customs, jealousies and rivalries, heuristics such as social proof, aims to become affiliated, avoidance of deviation and its potential consequences, or attempts to be successful, fashionable, distinctive, or legitimate, or to avoid pain. Imitation may lead to liking and mutual understanding. It may serve communicative intentions, such as approval or disapproval. In its effects, it may proliferate certain ways of acting through time thereby supporting a *status quo* in structures of power (Tarde, 1895/1903; Girard, 1972/1977; DiMaggio & Powell, 1983; Hurley & Chater, 2005; Bosch, 2016).

In competition, two or more parties to an interaction strive to achieve desired but scarce outcomes. The intensity and outcome of competition may depend on the significance of desired and undesired outcomes, the number of competitors, required and available resources, existing structures of power, the individual and collective power of participants, ways in which power is exercised, and strategies that are used. Competition may end when there are no more relevant desirable or undesirable outcomes left to compete for, when only one party remains, or when some agreement is reached among participants. Regulations and policies may exist to organize and limit the extent of competition. When competition intensifies, it can blend into conflict. Political competition is concerned with the attainment of positions of political power, policies, or outcomes. Economic competition refers to the attempt to gain economic advantages by creating and maintaining competitive advantage or by acquiring scarce goods or services. Social competition implies attempts at improving relative status positions. Thus, these different types of competition are oriented at gaining, consolidating, or enhancing sources of power that support positions in structures of power (Bosch, 2016).

In bargaining and negotiation, attempts are made by interacting parties to achieve agreement on issues of mutual concern to them. This may concern price levels of goods or services, contracts, policies, or anything else on which interests of parties may initially diverge. Various ways of exercising power may be used in the process, including coercion, inducement, manipulation, legitimation, and social influence techniques. Such ways of exercising power together with relevant structures of power, available individual and collective power, and strategies affect the outcome of the negotiation. In order to reach an agreement, a mediating party may be called in, or arbitration or litigation may be required. If no agreement is reached, a situation of conflict may result (Bosch, 2016; Mills, 2019).

Exchange implies reciprocal giving and receiving. This may refer to things, but it may also refer to one participant giving or doing something, and another doing something in return. Exchanges can occur on or off markets with exchange rates that may or may not be negotiable. They may be regulated by property rights and contract rules. Exchanges are influenced by available resources, calculations of costs, structures of power, the number of available exchange partners, the frequency of exchanges, and strategies used. As described in Chapter 2, the relative position of parties in exchanges indicates the extent of their economic power (Bosch, 2016).

Obedience refers to an interaction in which one party conforms to the commands of another. Such obedience can result from such factors as a lack of resources to resist, emotions such as fear and interest, shared goals or values, habits, customs, self-interest, a lack of knowledge, beliefs in legitimacy, a sense of duty, the presence of conformity values, a wish to avoid responsibility, or a general state of loss of control known as 'learned helplessness'. An act of obedience supports an existing structure of power (Bachrach & Baratz, 1963; Arendt, 1969; Olsen, 1970; Weber, 1922/1978; Schwartz et al., 2012; Bosch, 2016).

Resistance refers to an interaction in which an exercise of power by one party is counteracted by another. This may be an outcome of contrasting goals or values, feelings of lack of legitimacy, or the presence of self-direction or power values. An exercise of resistance implies an exercise of power, individually or collectively, with the possibility of using force, coercion, manipulation, authority, and legitimation and social influence techniques and supportive technology. Collective acts of resistance may include the exercise of pressure through discussion, negotiation, lobbying, or campaigning, the organization of protest or various types of collective action, or the forming of coalitions. Resistance can lead to changes in the way in which power is exercised by those against whom the resistance is oriented. It may also result in a subversion of existing structures of power, legislative actions, or exits from situations (Etzioni, 1968; Hirschman, 1970; Scott, 2001; Courpasson & Dany, 2009; Engelstad, 2009; Schwartz et al., 2012; Bosch, 2016).

Conflicts occur when antagonistic states exist or appear to exist between interests or actions of different parties. Types of conflict range from interpersonal to intergroup, ethnic, religious, international, or interclass conflict. Conflicts can become expressed in various ways, ranging from mild irritation to the extreme case of war. They may be or become enduring as a result of the existence or formation of antagonistic values, beliefs, or stereotypes. In conflicts, structures of power, individual and collective power, ways of exercising power, and strategies all impact on outcomes. Conflicts may be resolved through democratic means, regulation, authoritative decision-making, or interactive mechanisms such as diplomacy, mediation, negotiation, containment, or reconciliation procedures. Conflicts may also end when parties conclude that continuation of the conflict is less attractive than its conclusion. Other ways to resolve conflicts include the use of superordinate goals, the creation of interdependence, or the deployment of peace-keeping forces (Coser, 1961; Morgan, 1986; Bercovitch et al., 2009; Bosch, 2016).

As noted earlier, when interactions are oriented at common strategic goals, consciously or not, strategic interactions may be said to occur. To describe such strategic interactions, strategic scenarios may be developed. Simplified forms of strategic scenarios are provided by game theoretical models, which can be used in the development of actual strategic scenarios. Game theoretical models may be concerned with describing strategic competition, cooperation, coordination, deterrence, bargaining, and price-setting (Bosch, 2016).

A number of game theoretical models describe strategic competition. A zero-sum competitive game describes a situation in which rewards for one party imply losses for another – which affects the strategies that may be used. Entry deterrence and the dry cleaner game are zero sum games concerned with strategic interaction possibilities when a new party intends to enter a market threatening to take away profits from an incumbent. In this situation, the incumbent has several strategic options. A threat of or actual lowering of prices may deter the entry. If entry is allowed, lowering prices may make it harder for the entering party to survive but will be costly to the incumbent. Prices may also be kept stable, but this will lower profits for the incumbent. Finally, both the entrant and the incumbent may aim to differentiate products or services so as to maintain profits (Rasmusen, 2007; Andersen, 2013; Bosch, 2016).

The prisoner's dilemma game describes a situation in which two parties have to choose whether to perform a competitive action or a cooperative one. In the depicted situation, if one party competes and the other cooperates, the party that competes ends up with the highest rewards and the party that cooperates with the lowest. If both parties compete, they both end up with low, but not the lowest, rewards. If both parties cooperate, they end up with high, but not the highest, rewards. Which scenario is chosen may depend on the parties' attitudes to competition and cooperation, feelings about fair play and justice, tendencies to trust others, reputational concerns, and whether or not the situation is recurrent. If the situation is recurrent, various strategies may be used by parties, including grim (cooperate at first, then compete forever), tit-for-tat (start with cooperation, then respond in kind), minimax (try to keep rewards for the other party at a minimum), and maximin (maximize rewards when the other party uses minimax). A number of variations on the prisoner's dilemma game exist in which rewards are distributed slightly differently implying somewhat different strategic choices, as in the 'battle of the sexes'. Situations like that described by the prisoner's dilemma game include problems of collective action such as environmental protection (McCabe et al., 2001; Rasmusen, 2007; Andersen, 2013; Freedman, 2013; Bosch, 2016).

A number of games describe strategic coordination. The game of ranked coordination describes a situation in which performance of the same action by two parties leads to positive rewards while performance of different actions leads to negative rewards. If performed together, one type of action leads to higher rewards than another, implying that there is a need for a particular type of coordination. A number of games describe variations of this type of coordination. In 'the battle of the Bismarck Sea', one party is better off if actions differ, while the other party is better off if actions are the same. In the game of dangerous coordination, in one of the cases in which different actions are performed, there is a high negative reward for one party. The latter party will be strongly inclined to avoid that particular action. The welfare game describes a situation in which rewards are such that they make actions incompatible and coordination difficult. Coordination can result if one of the parties implements the strategy of follow-the-leader. Other coordination games, such as the game of duel, pay attention to the timing of actions and what this implies for coordination and rewards. Depending on the characteristics of real-life situations in which coordination is required, the different types of games of strategic coordination offer tools to draw up actual scenarios for such situations (Rasmusen, 2007; Bosch, 2016).

A situation of deterrence is described by the game of chicken. This game describes a situation in which parties mutually perform threatening actions. If one party gives in, rewards will be negative while rewards for the other party are positive. If neither party gives in, rewards are highly negative. If they both give in, rewards are limited. A sequence of chicken game scenarios over time is described by the 'war of attrition'. Here, outcomes depend on various strategies selected over time (Rasmusen, 2007; Freedman, 2013; Bosch, 2016).

A situation of bargaining is described by the trucking game. In this game, parties have to reach an agreement on how to share a particular road that can only be used by one party at a time while striving for rewards. The resulting rewards depend on which party has control over the road and which strategies are used. In the ultimatum game, control in bargaining lies fully in the hands of one party. The other party may either accept or decline the offers made. When there is a time limit, offers and counteroffers may lead the parties to settle for an agreement acceptable to both (Rasmusen, 2007; Watson, 2013; Bosch, 2016).

Price setting may also be described by games. In a Cournot game, two suppliers choose how much to produce based on price expectations, costs, and the potential production level of the other supplier. In a Bertrand model, suppliers choose prices based on the potential prices of the other supplier, and then determine how much to produce. A Hotelling game describes a situation in which suppliers choose locations and prices, a situation characteristic of monopolistic competition. Game theoretical models of auctions describe price bidding between buyers, where buyers estimate the value of products and the valuation of those products by other buyers. Depending on the procedures of the auction (sealed, ascending, descending), different strategies may be used (Rasmusen, 2007; Watson, 2013; Bosch, 2016).

Game theoretical models offer insights into relevant aspects of different types of strategic interaction in various situations, but they tend to be limited in complexity, scope, and applicability to real life. A more encompassing way to analyze (strategic) interaction is the use of scenarios. Such scenarios may include everything that may be of relevance to understand which interactions may occur in the future and what their effects may be. The development of scenarios starts with an understanding of the situation, or, in other words, with assessments. On the basis of such assessments, potential resources, goals, strategies, and implementation and action plans may be selected. Then, a new round of assessments is required to evaluate the potential impact of the action plans and potential changes in the situation as a result of changes in the social and natural environment. Multiple scenarios may be developed describing possible future interactions. When these scenarios are sufficiently elaborated, they can be used to actually prepare required resources, make goal-relevant decisions, choose appropriate strategies and implementation plans, and instigate actions. Whenever unexpected events occur, new scenarios can be drawn up. In the development of scenarios, various tools can be used in addition to those normally used for assessment as described earlier. Such tools include future-oriented interviews, questionnaires, brain storming sessions, role-playing, discussion groups, models, simulations, forecasts, and experiments (Hopkins & Zapata, 2007; Jiménez, 2010; Watson & Freeman, 2012; Bosch, 2016).

In the end, occurring interaction patterns express realized strategy – the actual strategy that turns out to have been implemented. In practice, much of planned strategy turns out not to be realized due to changes in social and natural environments, incorrect assessments or goal setting, ineffective strategies or implementations, unexpected strategic interactions, or incomplete scenarios. Much intended strategy therefore ends up as unrealized strategy (Mintzberg & Waters, 1985; Andersen, 2013).

Strategy and empowerment

It is hard to think of anything more empowering than a thorough understanding of strategy. And not just of one's own strategy, but especially of the potential strategies of others. If empowerment is taken to refer to actual abilities, then in practice, the use of abilities will depend on effective assessments, goal setting, choice of strategies, conscious or not, implementation, and interactions. Empowerment through knowledge of strategy works in multiple ways. It provides individual power due to the ability to understand how interaction works; it provides collective power because it allows for effective cooperation; it provides knowledge among opposing parties that may suggest constructive solutions to conflicts rather than destructive ones; and it offers insights that may undermine abusive uses of power.

References

Albright, S.C. & Winston, W.L. (2020). *Business analytics: Data analysis and decision making* (7th ed.). Boston, MA: Cengage.

Andersen, T.J. (2013). *Short introduction to strategic management.* Cambridge: Cambridge University Press.

Anderson, D., Wu, R., Cho, J.-S., & Schroeder, K. (2015). *E-government strategy, ICT and innovation for citizen engagement.* New York: Springer.

Ansoff, H.I. (1965). *Corporate strategy.* New York: McGraw-Hill.

Arendt, H. (1969). *On violence.* New York: Harcourt, Brace and World.

Atkinson, A.A., Kaplan, R.S., Matsumura, E.M., & Young, S.M. (2012). *Management accounting: Information for decision making and strategy execution* (6th ed.). Harlow: Pearson.

Bachrach, P. & Baratz, M. (1963). Decisions and nondecisions: An analytical framework. *American Political Science Review, 69*(3), 900–904. https://doi.org/10.2307/1952568.

Barney, J.B. & Hesterly, W.S. (2019). *Strategic management & competitive advantage* (6th ed.). New York: Pearson.

Bartholomees, J.B. Jr. (Ed.) (2012). *U.S. Army War College guide to national securities issues. Volume I: Theory of war and strategy* (5th ed.). Carlisle Barracks, PA: U.S. Army Strategic Studies Institute.

Bercovitch, J., Kremenyuk, V., & Zartman, I. (Eds.) (2009). *The SAGE handbook of conflict resolution.* Los Angeles, CA: SAGE.

Berthold, M.R., Borgelt, C., Höppner, F., Klawonn, F., & Silipo, R. (2020). *Guide to intelligent data science: How to intelligently make use of real data* (2nd ed.). Cham: Springer.

Bjerke, M.B. & Renger, R. (2017). Being smart about writing SMART objectives. *Evaluation and Program Planning, 61,* 125–127. https://doi.org/10.1016/j.evalprogplan.2016.12.009.

Bosch, R. (2016). *Power: A conceptual analysis.* The Hague: Eleven International Publishing.

Bourdieu, P. & Wacquant, L.J.D. (1992). *An invitation to reflexive sociology.* Cambridge: Polity Press.

Brantly, A.F. (2016). *The decision to attack: Military and intelligence cyber decision-making.* Athens, GA: The University of Georgia Press.

Burdon, M. (2020). *Digital data collection and information privacy law.* Cambridge: Cambridge University Press.

Clegg, S., Kornberger, M., Pitsis, T.S., & Mount, M. (2019). *Managing & organizations: An introduction to theory and practice* (5th ed.). Los Angeles, CA: SAGE.

Corea, F. (2019). *An introduction to data: Everything you need to know about AI, big data and data science.* Cham: Springer.

Coser, L.A. (1961). The termination of conflict. *The Journal of Conflict Resolution, 5*(4), 347–353. https://doi.org/10.1177/002200276100500401.

Courpasson, D. & Dany, F. (2009). Cultures of resistance in the workplace. In S.R. Clegg & M. Haugaard (Eds.), *The SAGE handbook of power* (pp. 332–347). Thousand Oaks, CA: SAGE.

Desai, M.A. (2019). *How finance works: The HBR guide to thinking smart about the numbers.* Boston, MA: Harvard Business Review Press.

DiMaggio, P.J. & Powell, W.W. (1983). The iron cage revisited: Institutional isomorphism and collective rationality in organizational fields. *American Sociological Review, 48*(2), 147–160. https://doi.org/10.2307/2095101.

Engelstad, F. (2009). Culture and power. In S.R. Clegg & M. Haugaard (Eds.), *The SAGE handbook of power* (pp. 210–238). Thousand Oaks, CA: SAGE.

Etzioni, A. (1968). *The active society: A theory of societal and political processes.* New York: The Free Press.

Fligstein, N. & McAdam, D. (2012). *A theory of fields.* New York: Oxford University Press.

Freedman, L. (2013). *Strategy: A history.* Oxford: Oxford University Press.

Freeman, R.E., Harrison, J.S., Wicks, A.C., Parmar, B.L., & De Colle, S. (2010). *Stakeholder theory: The state of the art.* Cambridge: Cambridge University Press.

Girard, R. (1972/1977). *Violence and the sacred* (P. Gregory, Trans.). Baltimore, MD: The Johns Hopkins University Press.

Goffman, E. (1961). *Encounters: Two studies in the sociology of interaction.* Indianapolis, IN: Bobbs-Merrill.

Grant, R.M. (2018). *Contemporary strategy analysis* (10th ed.). Hoboken, NJ: Wiley.

Gupta, D., Bhattacharyya, S., Khanna, A., & Sagar, K. (Eds.) (2020). *Intelligent data analysis: From data gathering to data comprehension.* Hoboken, NJ: Wiley.

Hall, P.A. & Soskice, D. (Eds.) (2001). *Varieties of capitalism: The institutional foundations of comparative advantage.* Oxford: Oxford University Press.

Harari, Y.N. (2019). *21 Lessons for the 21st Century.* London: Vintage.

Headquarters Department of the Army (2014). *Training circular no. 7–102: Operational environment and army learning.* Retrieved 31 January 2021, from https://armypubs.army.mil/epubs/DR_pubs/DR_a/pdf/web/tc7_102.pdf.

Hirschman, A.O. (1970). *Exit, voice, and loyalty: Responses to decline in firms, organizations, and states.* Cambridge, MA: Harvard University Press.

Hopkins, L.D. & Zapata, M.A. (Eds.) (2007). *Engaging the future: Forecasts, scenarios, plans, and projects.* Cambridge, MA: Lincoln Institute of Land Policy.

Hurley, S. & Chater, N. (Eds.) (2005). *Perspectives on imitation: From neuroscience to social science. Volume 2: imitation, human development, and culture.* Cambridge: The MIT Press.

Jiménez, J. (2010). How do scenario practices and search conferences complement each other? In R. Ramírez, J.W. Selsky, & K. Van der Heijden (Eds.), *Business planning for turbulent times: New methods for applying scenarios* (2nd ed.) (pp. 31–46). London: Earthscan.

Johanson, J.-E. (2019). *Strategy formation and policy making in government.* Cham: Palgrave Macmillan.

Lievrouw, L.A. (2018). Alternative computing. In G. Meikle (Ed.), *The Routledge companion to media and activism* (pp. 65–74). New York: Routledge.

Lin, H.L. & Zegart, A. (Eds.) (2019). *Bytes, bombs, and spies: The strategic dimensions of offensive cyber operations.* Washington, DC: Brookings Institution Press.

Littlejohn, S.W., Foss, Karen A., & Oetzel, J.G. (2017). *Theories of human communication* (11th ed.). Long Grove, IL: Waveland Press.

Machiavelli, N. (1519/1981). Discourses upon the first ten books of Titus Livy. In D. Donno (Trans.), *The prince* (pp. 91–122). New York: Bantam Books.

Machiavelli, N. (1532/2009). *The prince* (T. Parks, Trans.). London: Penguin Books.

Malesevic, S. (2009). Collective violence and power. In S.R. Clegg & M. Haugaard (Eds.), *The SAGE handbook of power* (pp. 274–290). Thousand Oaks, CA: SAGE.

McCabe, K.A., Rigdon, M.L., & Smith, V.L. (2001). Sustaining cooperation in trust games. *MPRA Paper*, 2006. Retrieved 11 April 2021, from https://mpra.ub.uni-muenchen.de/2006/.

Meikle, G. (Ed.) (2018). *The Routledge companion to media and activism.* New York: Routledge.

Mills, C.E. (2019). Negotiating. In O. Hargie (Ed.), *The handbook of communication skills* (4th ed.) (pp. 399–422). London: Routledge.

Mintzberg, H. & Waters, J.A. (1985). Of strategies, deliberate and emergent. *Strategic Management Journal, 6*(3), 257–272. https://doi.org/10.1002/smj.4250060306.

Morgan, G. (1986). *Images of organization.* Thousand Oaks, CA: SAGE.

Morton, J., Wilson, A., Galliers, R.D., & Marabelli, M. (2019). Open strategy and information technology. In D. Seidl, G. Von Krogh, & R. Whittington (Eds.), *Cambridge handbook of open strategy* (pp. 169–185). Cambridge: Cambridge University Press.

Nye, J.S. Jr. (2004). *Soft power: The means to success in world politics.* New York: Public Affairs.

Olsen, M.E. (1970). *Power in societies.* New York: Macmillan.

Pidun, U. (2019). *Corporate strategy: Theory and practice.* Wiesbaden: Springer Gabler.

Porter, M.E. (1980/1998). *Competitive strategy: Techniques for analyzing industries and competitors.* New York: The Free Press.

Porter, M.E. (1985). *Competitive advantage: Creating and sustaining superior performance.* New York: The Free Press.

Porter, M.E. (1990). *The competitive advantage of nations.* London: Macmillan

Porter, M.E. (2008). *On competition* (upd. & exp. ed.). Boston, MA: Harvard Business School Publishing.

Prahalad, C.K. & Hamel, G. (1990). The core competence of the corporation. *Harvard Business Review,* May–June, 79–91.

Prevos, P. (2019). *Principles of strategic data science: Creating value from data, big and small.* Birmingham: Packt Publishing.

Rasmusen, E. (2007). *Games and information: An introduction to game theory* (4th ed.). Malden, MA: Basil Blackwell.

Romney, M.B. & Steinbart, P.J. (2018). *Accounting information systems* (14th ed.). New York: Pearson.

Schwartz, S.H., Cieciuch, J., Vecchione, M., Davidov, E., Fischer, R., Beierlein, C., Ramos, A., Verkasalo, M.V., Lönnqvist, J.-E., Demirutku, K., Dirilen-Gumus, O., & Konty, M. (2012). Refining the theory of basic individual values. *Journal of Personality and Social Psychology, 103*(4), 663–688. https://doi.org/10.1037/a0029393.

Scott, J. (2001). *Power.* Cambridge: Polity.

Seidl, D., Von Krogh, G., & Whittington, R. (Eds.) (2019). *Cambridge handbook of open strategy.* Cambridge: Cambridge University Press.

Shah, C. (2020). *A hands-on introduction to data science.* Cambridge: Cambridge University Press.

Sharp, G. (2013). *How nonviolent struggle works.* East Boston, MA: The Albert Einstein Institution.

Sun, T. (6th cent. BC/1971). *The art of war* (S.B. Griffith, Trans.). Oxford: Oxford University Press.

Tarde, G. (1895/1903). *The laws of imitation* (E.C. Parsons, Trans.). New York: Henry Holt and Company.

Von Clausewitz, C. (1832/1989). *On war* (M. Howard & P. Paret, Eds. & Trans.). Princeton, NJ: Princeton University Press.

Watson, J. (2013). *Strategy: An introduction to game theory* (3rd ed.). New York: W.W. Norton & Company.

Watson, R. & Freeman, O. (2012). *Futurevision: Scenarios for the world in 2040.* Brunswick: Scribe Publications.

Weber, M. (1922/1978). *Economy and society* (G. Roth & C. Wittich, Eds.). Berkeley: University of California Press.

Williams, S. (2016). *Business intelligence strategy and big data analytics: A general management perspective*. Cambridge, MA: Elsevier.

Yarger, H.R. (2012). The strategic appraisal: The key to effective strategy. In J.B. Bartholomees, Jr. (Ed.), *U.S. Army War College guide to national securities issues. Volume I: theory of war and strategy* (5th ed.) (pp. 53–66). Carlisle Barracks, PA: U.S. Army Strategic Studies Institute.

6
COLLECTIVE POWER

Collective power may be said to exist when an ability exists for actions of different individuals to support each other through coordination or cooperation. Such an ability may exist between two people, in groups, organizations, coalitions, networks, or communities. In this chapter, these types of collective power will all be referred to as constituting an organization, as they all have some form of organization – whether or not explicitly so. In collective power, all the previously discussed categories of power are of importance. In other words, structures of power, individual power, exercises of power, and strategies all play a role. These take the forms of configurations of the formal and informal organization, organizational roles, individual psychology and behavior inside the organization, organizational social control, legitimation, and social influence processes, and internal strategies expressed in various internal policies. Collective power may empower those who form part of it, depending on their position in the organization. Knowledge about collective power may help to support its constructive rather than abusive use.

Structures of power in organizations

As described in Chapter 2, structures of power can be of various types. They may also have various configurations. When such configurations exist, some form of collective power exists of which they form a part. These configurations may be described in formal documents. If so, the descriptions constitute the formal organization of the collective power in question. In practice, configurations often diverge from their formal descriptions. The way configurations diverge from their formal descriptions is referred to as the informal organization. Configurations of

DOI: 10.4324/9781003034100-7

structures of power also indicate roles, which may be formal and/or informal. Formal and informal structures may support or undermine each other.

Formal organization

The formal organization consists of the design of an organization as reflected in official documents. Such documents may describe relationships among members of an organization, formal positions and roles, the distribution of authorities, responsibilities, and obligations, the allocation of tasks, spaces, and resources, coordination, cooperation, and participation procedures, and the constitution of organizational units and the relations between them. It may also include a code of ethics (Mintzberg, 1983; Bosch, 2016; Clegg et al., 2019).

A classical analysis of organizational design was presented by Mintzberg (1983), who described five ideal typical formal organizational configurations based on different ways in which constituting organizational parts are combined. The constituting parts distinguished by Mintzberg are the operating core – where the products or services are produced; the strategic apex – where top-level authority is located; the middle line – the hierarchy between the operating core and the strategic apex; the technostructure – analysts responsible for the standardization of activities; and the support staff – which provides services of various kinds not directly related to production. A first configuration based on these constituting parts is the simple structure, consisting of a small strategic apex and operating core with centralized direct supervision and little formalization and standardization. A more elaborate configuration is the machine bureaucracy. Here, the technostructure plays a key role, work processes and qualifications are standardized and formalized, and authority is organized in a centralistic, tall hierarchy. Another type of bureaucracy is the professional bureaucracy. In this configuration, the operating core is key, with specialized jobs based on standardized professional skills, relative autonomy of professionals, and an elaborate support staff. The fourth configuration is the divisionalized form. Here, the middle line is key, with its members heading vertically decentralized quasi-autonomous divisions with standardized outputs. The overall configuration is controlled by a small central strategic apex using divisional performance standards. The final configuration distinguished by Mintzberg is the adhocracy, in which the support staff is key, little formalization and standardization exists, jobs are specialized, work is organized in project teams, and decision-making is decentralized and often organized in a matrix structure combining authority of project managers with that of functional or departmental managers. These five ideal typical configurations do not exist as such in practice. They are analytical constructs that help in the analysis of actual formal organizational configurations (Weber, 1922). In practice, organizational configurations may resemble hybrids of the different configurations, with potential contradictions between constituting elements.

Additional potential structures and parts of structures of formal organization have been distinguished. The term flat structure has been used to refer to a formal organization in which the managerial hierarchy is small and much decision-making is decentralized. A small entrepreneurial structure has been said to exist when a lean and flexible structure is tightly controlled by an entrepreneur. A large entrepreneurial structure entails the existence of project teams and a flat structure with decentralized responsibilities and accountabilities. Network-based structures consist of relations between (quasi-)independent organizational units. In a boundaryless structure, formal cooperation exists with other organizations – as in joint ventures. A shamrock structure consists of a small core of permanent organizational members surrounded by a constantly changing contingent membership. In a heterarchy, organizational members are autonomous within a framework of agreed rules, democratic procedures, and mutual accountability. Finally, a virtual structure relies fundamentally on Information and Communications Technology (ICT) for its operation, to the extent that its members do not have to be in the same location to cooperate but can do so purely by means of ICT connections (Mintzberg, 1983; Ferlie & Pettigrew, 1996/1998; French et al., 2015; Bosch, 2016; Gómez-Mejía et al., 2016; Clegg et al., 2019).

Developments in ICT have led to an increase in organizational configurations that use digital platforms of various kinds as a basis for their operation. Such organizations may have conventional configurations with the digital platforms primarily serving as communication channels. But the use of digital platforms also allows for novel organizational configurations. One such configuration is that of holacracy, which consists of autonomous circles dedicated to particular functions that may overlap, dissolve, and develop depending on salient and novel projects and internal and external processes. Digitalization also facilitates the setting up of cooperative interfaces between different organizations, the geographical spreading of organizational activities, and the automation of organizational processes (Clegg et al., 2019).

Formal configurations may be organized according to functional departments, product, geographical or customer divisions, or projects. Matrix structures can exist that combine functional departments with divisional units with an intersection of a functional management and a divisional management layer. Formal organizational descriptions can show teams as components of an organization bound to particular hierarchical levels and/or organizational units, or cutting across such levels and/or units. Team members may be directly subordinated to a manager or supervisor, or a team may be relatively autonomous. Various types of teams can exist, ranging from project teams and problem-solving teams to quality control circles, special-purpose teams, and virtual/ICT-based teams. The relative power of individual organizational members, units, or teams within the formal structure depends on the organizational resources they can access as well as on their abilities to deal with critical contingencies for the organization. Formal job classification systems may exist that provide definitions and descriptions of jobs in terms of tasks, functions, duties, responsibilities, and required qualifications and skills. Jobs may be designed with various levels of complexity, specialization, team-orientation, and formal supervision. Formal processes of job rotation or job sharing may exist, implying the rotation or sharing of tasks among members of the organization (Hatch & Cunliffe, 2006; Clegg & Haugaard, 2012; French et al., 2015; Bosch, 2016; Gómez-Mejía et al., 2016).

Within organizations, various configurations of the production or service provision processes may exist. These include the job shop, where jobs are limited in scope, each with slightly different requirements; batch processing, where batches of goods or services are handled simultaneously; repetitive processing, where a high volume of standardized output is delivered; and continuous systems which process a high volume of non-discrete, highly standardized output. Repetitive processes and continuous systems frequently occur in organizational configurations with large hierarchies, extensive formalization and division of labor, and narrowly defined jobs. The design of such configurations is often based on a detailed analysis of workflows and human work abilities aimed at optimizing efficiency, an approach known as scientific management, Taylorism, or Fordism. An alternative way to organize work processes is through lean operations. In such operations, the aim is to deliver a variety of high quality goods or high quality services on the basis of broad jobs requiring a multi-skilled workforce working in teams with responsibility for just-in-time production, quality, and productivity (Taylor, 1911/1947; Womack et al., 1990; Clegg, 2009; Bosch, 2016; Stevenson, 2021).

Formal descriptions can also exist of governance structures. These include relations between owners/shareholders/voters and top managers/administrators, between an organization and other stakeholders such as financiers, governmental organizations, international legislative bodies, suppliers, customers, and communities, and between employers and employees. Owners/shareholders may own several organizations or have controlling shares in them. They can hold positions on administrative boards as independent or supervisory board members and formally delegate leadership or managerial roles, but they can also fulfill such roles themselves. Important financiers such as banks, venture capitalists, or various types of funds may own large blocks of shares and voting rights, provide credit, and fill seats on administrative boards. Other financiers can hold small amounts of shares or provide limited amounts of credit without much formal power. Governmental and international legislative bodies can hold formal power over organizations through formal legislation and policies. Formally described relationships may exist between organizations and suppliers, customers, and communities. Formal industrial relations structures can organize relations between employers and employees, both within individual organizations and nation-wide. This may include the existence of nation-wide employer organizations that represent employer interests and nation-wide unions that represent those of employees. Unions can also provide formal representation of employees at the enterprise level. Formal codetermination structures can exist that imply participation of employees in supervisory boards and/or works councils of organizations. Other formal structures for participation may exist, including elections and voting procedures, potentially supported by ICT platforms (Blanpain, 2014; Bosch, 2016; Clegg et al., 2019).

Overarching formal structures may exist, forming projects, conglomerates, or alliances. Formal configurations of state and societal structures can be distinguished, with variations in terms of the presence and configurations of constitutive institutions, including formal constitutions, formal electoral systems, legislatures, governmental systems and bureaucracies, party systems, legal and regulatory systems, markets, educational and vocational training institutions, and industrial relations systems. On the global level, formal treaties, intergovernmental organizations, and legal systems exist with various typologies (Hall & Soskice, 2001; French et al., 2015; Lansford, 2019; Caramani, 2020; Central Intelligence Agency, 2020).

A specific type of overarching formal structure is that constituted by the internet, which may be characterized as a global communication network based on supporting physical devices located in various jurisdictional areas. The position of an organization on the internet is based on relevant formal legislative authorities over (parts of) the internet as well as on sources of power discussed in Chapter 2, such as (ownership of) technological capabilities, available sources of finance, and market power (Winseck, 2019).

Informal organization

All relations between members of an organization that are not described in formal documents constitute the informal organization. This may include personal relations, social groups, coalitions, informal networks, and cultures (Barnard, 1938/1968). Personal relations can provide various types of support, including coordination or cooperation, which constitutes collective power.

Where more than two people are involved in personal relations with each other, and these people perceive themselves to constitute a group, an informal social group may be said to exist (Schein, 1988). Such groups may exist within the scope of an organization, organizational unit, or team, but they can also expand beyond these. Informal groups are often based on personal affinities, the existence of common backgrounds, aims, fears, norms, or habits, or needs for communion. Their members to some extent identify with each other, and this affects their goals and actions. This is strengthened by group peer pressures, groupthink (a striving for group unanimity that overrides a realistic appraisal of alternatives), group polarization (taking extreme positions to contrast with other groups), and in- and out-group bias (preferring members of one's group over others). All this potentially leads to a divergence with formal goals and desired actions of an organization, organizational unit, or team. But social groups may also identify with a particular organization, organizational unit, or team, and this may strengthen the collective power of the organization. Large organizations will tend to encompass various overlapping and conflicting groups which may or may not support the collective power of the organization as a whole. In such organizations, the power of a group depends on its constituting members and their positions and resources, as well as its size and cohesiveness (Selznick, 1957; French et al., 2015; Bosch, 2016; Clegg et al., 2019).

Coalitions may exist between social groups leading to some kind of mutual coordination or cooperation. Such coalitions may be based on the perception of shared goals, interests, values, or ideologies. In a sense, an informal organization as a whole can be seen as a coalition of groups with a stake in the organization. Together with formal groups, these stakeholder groups may include semi-formal groups such as financiers, managers, employees, government officials, customers, suppliers, social movements, and various other groups. In an organization, there is often a dominant coalition centered around a top-level manager or other key organizational member(s) that holds the power to strongly affect organizational actions (Selznick, 1957; Morgan, 1986; Bosch, 2016; Clegg et al., 2019).

Another type of informal organization consists of informal networks of relationships that relate individuals, groups, or organizations to each other in a loose fashion. Such networks can be based on contacts through such factors as geographical locations, work or leisure activities, resource dependencies, or intermediaries. Several types of networks have been distinguished based on the type of resource that is exchanged in the network. An exchange network is a network in which products or services are exchanged; in communication networks, there is an exchange of information; in social networks, there is an exchange of affections and opinions; and in communities of practice networks, there is an exchange and development of knowledge. As in the case of organizational typologies, distinguishing types of networks can help in analyzing actual networks even if in reality these will tend to contain aspects of multiple types. Geography-based networks may constitute industrial clusters – networks of organizations that compete and cooperate with each other at the same time. Networks of organizations and organizational units may also be included in overarching projects. When networks become linked to other networks, they can become wide-reaching or global in scope. Internally, networks may vary in interconnectedness, complexity, and the centrality of its members. It is such centrality, as well as mediating positions, resource dependencies, and links to other networks that constitute sources of power for members in the network. Externally, powerful networks can exist among top-level officials of different organizations as a result of multiple top-level positions, common backgrounds, or family ties. Such powerful networks may stimulate the pursuit of similar objectives and common strategies. They can support the spread of organizational configurations, practices, norms, values, and identities (Porter, 1998; Wenger, 1998; Smith-Doerr & Powell, 2005; Castells, 2010; Clegg & Haugaard, 2012; Sinclair, 2012; Bosch, 2016).

In the broadest sense, culture refers to 'webs of significance spun by man', with meanings dependent on interpretation (Geertz, 1973, p. 5). Shared webs of significance, that is, shared cultures, may exist with various scopes and strengths, reaching from small groups to wide regions of the globe, and from weak to strong cultures. Understanding shared webs of significance focuses on the interpretation of social elements of culture, such as interpretive frames, interaction patterns, language, symbols, rituals, myths, stories, and taken-for-granted aspects of social life. This leads to an understanding of social life as negotiation and accomplishment, and a recognition of the importance of the situational context. Culture considered this way is specific to place and time, and should be understood and analyzed as such (Goffman, 1959; Garfinkel, 1967; Geertz, 1973; Hatch & Cunliffe, 2006).

Another approach to culture has focused on shared individual psychological tendencies, such as values, beliefs, attitudes, and ideas. In a well-known study taking this type of approach, based on survey questions and statistical analyses to measure psychological tendencies, Hofstede et al. (2010) distinguished six dimensions of national culture. The first is power distance. A high statistical score on this dimension among people surveyed in a country is taken to indicate that expectance and acceptance of an unequal distribution of power is high. The second dimension suggested by Hofstede et al. is that of individualism versus collectivism. When a high score is obtained for individualism, ties between individuals are thought to be loose, with everyone expected to look only after him- or herself and immediate family. When instead a high score is found for collectivism, people in a country are thought to be integrated into strong cohesive in-groups, providing protection in exchange for loyalty. The third dimension is masculinity versus femininity. A high score on masculinity is interpreted to indicate a national culture where men are supposed to be assertive, tough, and focused on material success and women are expected to be modest, tender, and concerned with the quality of life. Reversely, a culture with a high score on femininity is thought to be one in which both men and women supposed to be modest, tender, and concerned with the quality of life. The fourth dimension, uncertainty avoidance, refers to the "extent to which the members of a culture feel threatened by ambiguous or unknown situations" (Hofstede et al., 2010, p. 191, emphasis in the original). The fifth dimension is long-term versus short-term orientation. When a high score is found on long-term orientation, a culture is thought to foster virtues such as perseverance and thrift which are oriented toward future rewards. In contrast, when a high score is found on short-term orientation, a culture is thought to foster virtues such as respect for tradition, preservation of face, and the fulfillment of social obligations, which are seen to be related to the past and present. The final dimension distinguished by Hofstede et al. is that of indulgence versus restraint. A high score on indulgence is thought to indicate a tendency toward allowing the gratification of desires related to enjoying life, whereas a high score on restraint is seen to reflect a conviction that such gratification needs to be restricted and regulated by social norms.

Taking a similar approach but focusing on cultures of organizations, Hofstede et al. (2010) suggest six dimensions. In their interpretation, organizational cultures may be distinguished on the basis of the extent to which they are process-oriented versus results oriented, employee- oriented versus job-oriented, parochial versus professional, open versus closed, having loose versus tight control, and being normative versus pragmatic.

Schwartz (2007) argued that measurements of individual scores on values provide an indication of national culture when aggregated and statistically interpreted. This implies that the value types distinguished by Schwartz et al. (2012), which were discussed in Chapter 3, are seen to allow for an interpretation of national culture. Thus, in this view, national cultures may be assessed based on scores on the value dimensions of self-protection and avoiding anxiety versus anxiety-free growth, personal outcomes versus social outcomes, self-transcendence versus self-enhancement, and conservation versus openness to change.

Using outcomes of the 'World Values Survey' which also surveys individuals, Inglehart argued for the existence of two dimensions of culture: traditional versus secular-rational orientations toward authority and survival versus self-expression values. Traditional orientations toward authority are thought to be expressed in obedience to religious authority, adherence to communal obligations, and the relevance attached to sharing. Secular-rational orientations are seen to imply that authority is considered legitimate on rational–legal grounds, and that an emphasis is placed on individual achievement and economic wealth. A presence of survival values are thought to indicate the importance of hard work and self-denial, whereas self-expression values are seen to include an emphasis on the quality of life, emancipation, and self-expression. According to Inglehart, economic development has led to a shift from traditional and survival values toward secular-rational and self-expression values (Bosch, 2016; Inglehart, 2018).

Schein (2010) sees culture as constituted by unconscious, taken-for-granted beliefs and values that determine behaviors, perceptions, thoughts, and feelings. These taken-for-granted beliefs and values become expressed in ideals, goals, values, aspirations, ideologies, rationalizations, and artifacts. A number of dimensions of taken-for-granted beliefs and values are seen to exist, indicating differences between macrocultures of nations, ethnic and religious groups, and globally occurring occupations. These dimensions are concerned with the nature of reality and truth, time, space, human nature, human activity, and human relationships. Schein distinguished three organizational subcultures: an operator culture oriented toward doing the job, an engineer culture concerned with innovation, and an executive culture focused on maintaining economic health (Bosch, 2016).

The approach to culture based on shared individual psychological tendencies tends to ignore the relevance of structures and exercises of power, conflict, and other social factors that play a role in constituting culture. In its turn, the social interpretive approach to culture tends to be situationally and temporally specific, which limits the development of general insights that can be widely used for interpretation. An empowering approach is to see research into shared individual psychological tendencies as providing interpretive tools that may be helpful in cultural interpretation together with situational and temporal interpretation of social elements of culture (Bosch, 2016).

Contradictions may exist within and between informal organizations. They may also provide support to or be at variance with formal organizations. Support for formal organizations can result from such elements of informal organization as support for authority, work motivation, self-discipline, and the provision of informal communication channels. Reversely, conflicting goals, loyalties, and identities may contradict formal organization (French et al., 2015; Bosch, 2016; Gómez-Mejía et al., 2016).

Roles

Roles are behavior patterns connected to positions in social structures. The meaning of particular roles depends on existing interpretations, as does their enactment. Roles may contain contradictory elements and overlap or conflict with other roles. As with other elements of structure, roles are never completely stable as they depend on ever changing interpretations. There are as many roles as there are positions in social structures. This section will focus on three powerful roles: the managerial, the entrepreneurial, and the leadership roles.

In his classic *The function of the executive*, Barnard (1938/1968) distinguished three main components of the managerial role: to promote the securing of essential efforts; to provide a system of communication; and to formulate and define purpose. In order to promote the securing of efforts and provide a system of communication, the formal and information organization needs to be designed. Organizing the manner in which members of organizations are recruited, promoted, trained, and dismissed is another way to promote the securing of efforts, as is the installment of an incentive system. Various social control techniques may be used including sanctioning, the use of authority, divide and conquer, and the use of technology. Decision-making, delegation, participation, appraisal, and conflict management systems can be set up. Legitimation and social influence and socialization techniques may also be used (Selznick, 1957; Beer et al., 1984; Morgan, 1986; Bosch, 2016; Gómez-Mejía et al., 2016; Clegg et al., 2019). Formulating and defining purpose forms part of the development of strategies for an organization, which – as discussed in the previous chapter – also includes assessment, the development of strategic approaches, the implementation of strategic courses of action, and strategic interactions. For an organization, this also implies networking and balancing the interests of various internal and external stakeholders in the organization (Freeman et al., 2010; Bosch, 2016).

The entrepreneurial role is concerned with turning novel ideas or inventions into innovations. In a classical analysis, Kanter (1988) distinguished four steps to achieve this: idea generation and selection, coalition building around the innovation project in which resources are allocated, idea realization by a project team, and transfer to those who will embody or exploit the innovation. This process can be routinized by setting up R&D and innovation centers. The entrepreneurial role also entails designing formal and informal structures supportive of innovations, developing an innovation strategy, handling legal issues and the institutional environment, and collaborating and competing with those performing entrepreneurial roles in other organizations (Van de Ven & Hargrave, 2004; Bessant & Tidd, 2015; Bosch, 2016; Clegg et al., 2019).

According to Kotter's (1990/1998) classical statement, the leadership role is concerned with coping with change. It includes the development of a vision for an organization together with strategies to achieve it, the alignment of people with that vision through communication, and the motivation and inspiration of people to act accordingly. The leadership role has also been seen to include setting the example by means of public actions, implementing policies consistent with the vision, and such activities as building coalitions, performing negotiations, balancing the interest of stakeholders, deciding, directing, monitoring, controlling, coaching, mentoring, and supporting, and dealing with conflict. A leadership role may be formal or informal, and for a small group of people or a large organization (Selznick, 1957; Gordon, 2002; Schein, 2010; Haslam et al., 2011; French et al., 2015; Bosch, 2016; Clegg et al., 2019).

Individual power within organizations

Individual power within collective power in the first place depends on the positions of individuals in the structure of collective power. This may refer to formal positions in the organization in terms of hierarchical management levels or functions, but also to informal positions in terms of social power resulting from social status, strategic expertise, access to critical resources, or powerful connections (Clegg et al., 2019). Particular positions in a structure of collective power may lead to similarities in psychological characteristics to others in similar positions, alongside idiosyncratic psychological characteristics.

Those who fulfill a leadership or managerial role can derive considerable individual power from their position in a formal or informal organization. On the basis of the way in which they express such power in their behavior, a number of types of leadership have been distinguished. In a classical analysis, McGregor (1960) distinguished between Theory X and Theory Y. According to Theory X, people dislike work and prefer to be directed. A leadership style in line with these ideas is based on coercion and direction. According to Theory Y, work comes natural to people, and people like to take responsibility and be creative. A leadership style in line with Theory Y includes the use of inducement, delegation, and participation. Related to this, according to Bass and Bass (2008), an important dichotomy in styles of leadership is that between autocratic versus democratic. An autocratic leadership style focuses on giving directions, tasks to be performed, and the exercise of control. It may be abusive and violent. A democratic leadership style allows for participation and delegation and has a relationship orientation. Bass and Bass also suggest the existence of an important dichotomy between transactional leadership, which focuses on the exchange relation with followers, and transformational leadership, which aims to stimulate and satisfy a large spectrum of needs of followers. A distinction can also be made between active leaders who take responsibility for decisions, and laissez-faire leaders who do not. Different traits have been attributed to leaders, ranging from task accomplishment traits such as intelligence, experience, intuition, and knowledge, to interpersonal competence traits such as the ability to communicate and to demonstrate caring, insight, and empathy. Traits that are seen as deleterious to leadership include neuroticism, arrogance, anxiety, depression, narcissism, and rigidity. Transformational leaders are thought to be charismatic and inspirational (Bass & Bass, 2008).

Other members of an organization also derive a certain amount of power from their formal or information positions. Their individual power also depends on the values and attitudes they hold with regard to their roles and behaviors in the organization. Four types of work-related values have been distinguished: intrinsic values, referring to the goals of interesting, varied, and autonomous work; extrinsic values, including good salary and working conditions, and job security; social values, including contributing to, working with others, and social contact with co-workers; and prestige/power values, including the authority to make decisions over people, and prestigious, highly valued work. Attitudes toward work may differ in terms of the extent to which it is seen as having to be useful, obligatory, varied, and financially rewarding, provide job and pay security, and offer career opportunities or meaningful relations with colleagues. The work-related values and attitudes individuals hold may or may not be similar to those expressed or supported by the formal and/or informal organization, and the management practices in the organization. Where values and/or attitudes are similar, an individual may feel empowered by the organization and vice versa, whereas if values and/or attitudes differ, conflicts may occur or the individual may maintain an instrumental view of organizational membership in service of other non-work-related purposes. Whether or not individuals will hold instrumental views of organizational membership also depends on their trust in the organization and their satisfaction with their work. This affects absenteeism and exit from the organization, as well as their identification with and commitment and loyalty to the organization – which influences both their individual power as well as the collective power of the organization (Ros et al., 1999; Bosch, 2016).

In their thinking process, individuals give meaning to their encounters with organizational characteristics. They may react in varied ways to exercises of power within organizations. Whereas some individuals may respond to social control with obedience and to legitimation and social influence practices by internalizing promoted views, others may resist. Some individuals may obey out of respect for authority, others may do so out of fear for sanctions. Individuals may also vary in their work engagement, that is, the extent to which they invest personal energies into their work. People may or may not identify with their work, professional group, or organization, which affects their behavior in and on behalf of organizations in terms of task performance and productivity. They may differ in the extent to which their individual power is adjusted by technologies – as discussed in Chapter 3 (Weick, 1995; Bardon et al., 2012; Bosch, 2016; Clegg et al., 2017; Robbins & Judge, 2018).

Individuals in organizations can differ significantly in individual characteristics. Diversity in individual characteristics has been seen to stimulate creativity, improve problem-solving, enhance flexibility, and provide a broader availability of information. But differences in psychological characteristics can also lead to misunderstandings, conflicts, stereotyping, and discrimination (Gómez-Mejía et al., 2016; Clegg et al., 2019).

ICT has allowed people to work from anywhere as 'digital nomads', as long as they have access to the internet and can do their jobs online rather than having to be at a particular place in person (Clegg et al., 2019). As discussed in Chapter 3, ICT has also extended individual capabilities of organizational members through various techno-adjustments. The use of automatization, data science, AI, and robotics has also led to a shift in tasks for organizational members (West, 2018).

Exercising power within organizations

The way in which power is exercised within collective power by those in positions of power has been referred to as 'governance'. This process includes various social control, legitimation, and social influence processes as described in Chapter 4. Together they may be seen to constitute what Foucault referred to as government or governmentality, including biopower and disciplinary power as described in Chapter 2.

Social control in organizations

A first important social control technique used within collective power is that of force. In the form of violence, force can be used to exclude people from an organization in various ways, ranging from impeding them to take part in the organization to murdering them. It may also be used to keep people inside organizations by restraining them from leaving. Yet another use of violence in organizations is the execution of punishment. Violence can also be used to instill fear in those organizational members not directly subject to it. It may also result from emotional upheaval or the fulfilment of violent desires. Other types of force include the performance of physical labor that contributes to interpersonal or organizational goals such as construction work or the provision of care, and constructive forces exerted by machines (Bosch, 2016).

Various types of coercion can occur within organizations, including the threat of the use of force or punishments such as termination, demotion, or the withholding of resources, efforts, or rewards. Coercion is a central element of discipline, which consists of the direction, supervision, surveillance, and codification of activities, and the communication of warnings or execution of punishments for undesired behaviors. Such discipline may encourage organizational members to monitor their own behaviors, which implies processes of self-coercion. Coercion can also be embodied in used technologies and building designs. Non top level members of organizations may also use coercion in various ways, including underperformance, (threats of) exit, legal action, and union activities (Hardy & Clegg, 2006; Bosch, 2016; Gómez-Mejía et al., 2016).

The use of inducement as a social control technique in organizations is ubiquitous. A first expression of such use is existing reward systems, which may include pay, benefits, and nonfinancial rewards. Pay may be a fixed amount in a certain time period based on the power to determine pay, hierarchical position, job demands, skills, expertise, seniority, and responsibilities. It may also be based on historical wage patterns, pay for similar jobs in other organizations, legislation, organizational politics, pressures by employee representatives, and a willingness to pay. Pay can also be variable and dependent on individual, team, unit, or organization-wide performance. Such performance-based pay systems aim to tie (collective) self-interest to the results of the organization to induce desired behaviors. Typical forms of individual performance-related pay include piece-rate systems, commission systems, bonus plans, and merit pay. Team, unit, or organization-wide performance related pay systems include such systems as profit sharing, gain sharing, bonuses, and employee stock or options. Nonfinancial rewards such as recognition, praise, and the delegation of authority may also be used in an attempt to enhance commitment, cooperation, and performance. Inducements can also be provided through the enlargement, enrichment, or rotation of jobs, and the provision of job security, career paths, and education. Delegation of or participation in decision-making can also be used to enhance motivation, as can the stimulation of good relations with direct management, clear, meaningful, and attainable goals, and a clear linkage of action to valued outcomes. Counseling sessions may be provided as a way to induce members to adjust behaviors, as may other techniques of 'organizational compassion' such as the presence of a harm notification network. For effective inducement, incentives provided should not undermine intrinsic motivation, and rewards should be clearly linked to performance (Barnard, 1938/1968; Beer et al., 1984; Hardy & Clegg, 2006; Simpson et al., 2014; Bosch, 2016; Gómez-Mejía et al., 2016; Clegg et al., 2019).

Coercion can be used in combination with inducement in the form of formal and informal rules that may or may not contradict each other. Formal rules underlie the formal organization with its designation of positions, roles, authorities, accountabilities, resources, relationships, procedures, incentive systems, technologies, and its organization of the production or service provision processes. Such formal designations both restrict and enable behavioral possibilities thereby allowing social control. Certain authorities and accountabilities can be centralized to enhance positions of power from which social control can be exercised. Hierarchies may be set up to establish social control through intermediate managerial levels. Other authorities may be delegated, formally separated, or shared, effecting a division of powers or participation through formal description. Voting procedures can be used to allow for an extent of bottom-up social control. Standardization and formalization of activities may enhance control, as may the use of formal teams and job descriptions. Formal procedures can exist for the establishment of membership of organizations. Certain memberships may be made obligatory, such as national citizenship, compulsory schooling, or slavery. In businesses, formal staffing procedures may be used for recruitment, career development, training, and separation, and employment or commercial contracts. Such procedures may be subject to encompassing regulations, such as those by governmental or international organizations. These procedures and rules restrict how membership can be achieved, developed, and ended while at the same time providing inducements to operate in line with established procedures. Other formal regulations can exist in the field of remuneration, setting standards and limits to the distribution of rewards among members. Formal arrangements of governance may regulate relations between top management and various stakeholders. Decision making rules can affect how decisions in an organization are reached. Formal procedures for classification, observation, notation, accounting, examination, analysis, and assessment all have implications in terms of social control, in what they enforce and stimulate. Formal disciplinary rules indicate acceptable and unacceptable behaviors (Weber, 1922/1978; Mintzberg, 1983; Scott, 1994; Hatch & Cunliffe, 2006; Clegg & Haugaard, 2012; Bosch, 2016).

Informal rules also combine coercion with inducement by means of normative pressures that express critique or support. In organizations, such informal rules result from the norms that organizational members hold individually and as groups, and from the interactions that take place among them. Informal routines, procedures, and assumptions also effect social control. They may play a role in concertive control, where a sense of responsibility to other team members leads to a control over behavior. Like formal rules, informal rules both restrict and enable certain types of actions. They play a role alongside formal rules in the way in which membership of an organization is established and developed, rewards are distributed, relations between management and stakeholders are arranged, and decisions and coordination are established through informal communication. They also influence the actual functioning of formal procedures concerned with classification, accounting, assessment, surveillance, and discipline. Formal and informal rules may also be invoked by organizational members to protect themselves against work intensification (Mintzberg, 1983; Barker, 1993; Bosch, 2016; Clegg et al., 2019; Sewell, 2021).

The use of divide and conquer in organizations may imply a division of structures of power. When this is done vertically, different layers of governance are separated from each other, as is done in federalist organizational structures. Horizontal divisions of structures of power imply the attribution of different activities to distinct components, as in the separation of legislative, judicial, and administrative activities. Organizational members can be divided by creating hierarchical levels or separate units. Job descriptions and physical segregation may aim at dividing structures of power at lower hierarchical levels. Groups can be specifically created to break up pre-existing groups in order to attain support for particular policies. Employee groups can be divided by giving them different employment statuses, such as regular versus contingent employment. External hiring brings new people into an organization which may break up (potential) collaborations between members. Promotion policies can be used to coopt potentially antagonistic members, and reward policies can encourage competition rather than collaboration. A limited extent of participation of organizational members in decision-making can be set up to diffuse opposition. Implementing policies that discriminate between groups of members can lead to differences in terms of positions, resources, career opportunities, and rewards. To overcome divisions of power, alliances may be formed among internal members or with external stakeholders and groups (Morgan, 1986; Courpasson, 2000; Poggi, 2001; Keister & Southgate, 2012; Bosch, 2016).

Deception can be used in various ways to achieve control, including intentional miscommunication, fraud, and corruption. Heresthetic techniques may be used such as agenda control, the setting of deadlines, strategic voting, and the discursive manipulation of dimensions to control organizational decision-making. Symbolic or theatrical behavior can also enhance internal social control (Hatch & Cunliffe, 2006; Castells, 2009; Bosch, 2016). A notorious impact of ICT is the possibility it allows for deception through the spread of 'fake news', facilitated by the ease of posting online and the willingness to believe by anyone so inclined. Compared to other methods of deception, ICT allows reaching a large audience very quickly including members of a particular organization (Greifeneder et al., 2021).

Authority is used extensively in organizations to maintain control. Such authority can derive from organizational positions, expertise, personal characteristics or contacts, or any of the other sources of authority discussed in Chapter 2. It supports giving commands as well as the making of decisions. Decision making authority may be centralized and top-down but it can also be delegated or allow for participation. Delegation can extend the reach of overarching authority, while stimulating support from those to whom authority is delegated. Processes of participation may allow organizational members to participate directly or through representation or voting mechanisms. Such participation may be organized formally through representation on committees, councils, or through codetermination on company boards. Stock ownership may also allow some participation based on ownership shares or voting rights, as may participation in project teams or quality control circles. Unions and elected works council representatives also provide more or less formal forms of participation. Participation can also be informal in the form of pressure or lobbying groups or network relations. The existence of participation may enhance cooperation and organizational performance and reduce conflict, but when it is conceived as deceptive or ineffective, it may backlash and cause conflicts. In addition, organizational members in position of power may feel threatened, hampering the implementation of effective processes of participation (Kochan & Osterman, 1994/1998; Courpasson, 2000; Wilkinson et al., 2013; Bosch, 2016; Gómez-Mejía et al., 2016).

Another social control technique in organizations consists of codification of knowledge, surveillance, and appraisal. Behaviors, performance, attitudes, qualifications, and competences may be observed, measured, classified, and registered.

The use of IT-systems allows for extensive development and storage of knowledge as well as for arm's-length surveillance and appraisal. The results of such appraisal can form the basis for other social control techniques such as coercion, discipline, reward policies, and the use of authority. It may motivate organizational members but it may also undermine morale and lead to conflicts when unclear standards are used, differences between organizational members become emphasized, appraisal is performed incorrectly or very subjectively, or surveillance and appraisal mostly appear to serve the purposes of the powerful. Appraisers too may experience drawbacks with the use of appraisal systems. To avoid conflicts or unwanted use of appraisal data, they may give positive evaluations to all surveilled organizational members who, in their turn, may engage in various forms of deceptive activities to avoid negative appraisals (Foucault, 1975/1977; Clegg, 1989; Bach, 2013; Randall & Sim, 2014; Bosch, 2016; Gómez-Mejía et al., 2016; Clegg et al., 2019; Sewell, 1998, 2021).

Communication is yet another technique for social control. It can be used to provide information on organizational goals, to instruct other organizational members, to provide information on tasks, to provide feedback, and to gather information. Extensive communication can support decision-making and the implementation of strategies. It may support commitment, participation, and the impact of other social control techniques. It can be facilitated by IT systems, but IT systems can also be used to restrict, censor, or surveil communications. Communications may provide relevant information, but they also allow for the use of deception (Engelstad, 2009; French et al., 2015; Bosch, 2016; Gómez-Mejía et al., 2016; Clegg et al., 2019; Sewell, 2021).

A number of typologies of control systems have been distinguished that combine different ways of exercising control. In a bureaucratic control system, social control is attained by designing the formal organization in the form of a hierarchy, with extensive ascriptions to positions of tasks, resources, authorities, and responsibilities. Formal rules and regulations are used to describe work behaviors, employment, reward, and training systems, career paths, surveillance, appraisal, and disciplinary policies. A classical example of an application of a bureaucratic control system is scientific management. In scientific management, the formal organization and formal rules ascribe decision-making, organization, and planning to managerial positions and strict, narrow tasks to unskilled workers. Tasks to be performed as well as the abilities of workers are analyzed in detail, a process referred to as 'scientific'. Task-specific training is provided. Tasks are to be performed under strict systems of surveillance, appraisal, and discipline, with rewards depending on performance. Bureaucratic control systems can enhance performance when work is simple and repetitive. But they can also lead to the exercise of petty tyranny, alienation, absenteeism and turnover, low quality work, low innovation, and labor conflicts (Taylor, 1911/1947; Mintzberg, 1983; Ashforth, 1994; Bahnish, 2000; Courpasson & Clegg, 2006; Hatch & Cunliffe, 2006; Clegg, 2009; Bosch, 2016).

Other types of control systems include corporatist, market, entrepreneurial, and patronal control. Corporatist control systems have extensive hierarchies that contribute to social control by providing inducements to achieve promotions, dividing groups, and allowing the exercise of authority. In this control system, self-managing teams support concertive control, career paths are offered to core workers, certain mechanisms for participation in decision-making exist, and job enrichment is used providing intrinsic rewards. Socialization practices create dependencies and aim to enhance commitment. In market-based control systems, members are recruited when they are needed and let go when this is no longer the case. On their side, members may leave when they are dissatisfied, as their commitment to the organization is low. In an entrepreneurial control system, organizational members are stimulated to be creative, autonomous, and proactive. Competition between groups is stirred up, while at the same time quality control and communication groups are used to support quality and coordination. Patronal control may exist in small organizations with an owner-manager running an organization as if it were a family (Du Gay & Salaman, 1992; Courpasson & Clegg, 2006; Pendleton & Gospel, 2013; Bosch, 2016).

Another type of control may be said to exist in total institutions. Here, social control is encompassing with members cut off from the rest of society. In such institutions, members are regimented, often wear specific uniforms, and daily life is strictly organized in time. Surveillance is continuous and conformity is expected to existing rules. This type of control can be found in various organizations ranging from schools and hospitals to prisons and concentration camps (Clegg et al., 2019).

Social control techniques may be resisted individually or collectively by a lack of compliance, attempts at participation, or exits from the organization. Countervailing coalitions can be built to influence the ways in which social control is exerted. Such resistance can lead to contradictions or conflicts. It may also incite competition between members for positions, remunerations, or educational possibilities. Conflicts may also arise due to technological changes, financial problems for the organization, or regarding regulations, organizational policies, and management styles. Attempts can be made to resolve such conflicts on the basis of conflict resolution procedures, including due process, grievance procedures, discussions, mediation, or bargaining (Hirschman, 1970; Barbalet, 1985; Morgan, 1986; Hardy & Clegg, 2006; Hatch & Cunliffe, 2006; French et al., 2015; Bosch, 2016).

Legitimation in organizations

The design of the formal organization may support legitimation, as when particular formal structures are chosen because of their discursive legitimacy. Such legitimate formal structures are meant to provide meaning and purpose to members in the organization. Their legitimacy may be due to their apparent presence in organizations that are seen as successful, because they are in line with governmental regulations, or because they are seen as rational or progressive. Professions, products and services, technologies, strategies, programs, ethical rules, and policies can all serve mythical roles in establishing legitimacy and they may be adopted ceremonially. Externally, such legitimacy facilitates the acquisition of resources and organizational members, the conduct of exchanges, and the winning of contracts and subsidies. Internally, legitimacy supports the commitment and compliance of organizational members (Powell & DiMaggio, 1991; Bosch, 2016). As part of the formal organization, hierarchy can provide legitimation for a large overall difference in authority. This is because layering relationships hierarchically provides authority to those occupying positions at various managerial levels while reducing inequality between the levels. This way a large overall difference in authority can be legitimated by referring to existing delegation and responsibilities (Poggi, 2001).

Employment and reward policies may also support legitimacy. Internal recruitment and the offering of career paths and education possibilities can provide legitimacy to organizational authority, as can the recruitment of top talent. Reward policies can legitimate certain types of authority based on the criteria used in compensation, which may range from performance to merit, seniority, hierarchical position, experience, knowledge, or wages on labor markets. Making distinctions in benefits provided to various groups of employees may symbolize hierarchy, thereby reinforcing the idea of the legitimacy of hierarchy. Other social control techniques such as formal rules, goal setting, and accounting, appraisal, surveillance, and disciplinary procedures may also legitimate authority due to the principles on which they are based (O'Neill, 1986; Hatch & Cunliffe, 2006; Bosch, 2016).

Discourses can be used to attain legitimating meanings, categories, labels, frames, and understandings, including what is considered normal and abnormal, just and unjust, appropriate and inappropriate. They may aim to reify structures of power, individual powers, and exercises and strategies of power. Ideologies can also serve to legitimate authorities within an organization. Overarching organizational ideologies may include systems of ideas regarding shareholder value orientation, customer orientation, excellence, empowerment, consensus, survival, sustainability, and egalitarianism. Ideologies of merit, tradition, or natural, religious, or social superiority may legitimate internal structures of power and differences in positions. In its turn, an ideology of equality can undermine such legitimation. Decisions and actions can be legitimated by means of metaphors, or knowledge or ethical claims. The discursive constitution of what is to be considered normal may legitimate regulations and disciplinary practices (Gramsci, 1971; Foucault, 1975/1977, 1980; Courpasson, 2000; Hardy et al., 2000; Mumby, 2004; Grusky et al., 2008; Clegg & Haugaard, 2012; Bosch, 2016; Clegg et al., 2019).

Various symbols, myths, and stories can be used to legitimate authority and policies in an organization. Reports, practices, models, dress codes, key leaders, exemplary organizational units, flags, and logos may be used as symbols to establish legitimacy. Myths can be created of natural or supernatural rights to authority. Myths of the existence and implementation of particular overall management systems can legitimate authorities and policies. Themes of excellence, sacrifice, and justice may be invoked to stimulate performance or implement change. Symbols, myths, or stories can also be used to depersonalize or dehumanize resisting forces (O'Neill, 1986; Powell & DiMaggio, 1991; Mumby, 2004; Clegg et al., 2013; Freedman, 2013; Bosch, 2016).

Ritual ceremonies such as rites of passage can be used to legitimate changes in social positions or status and reinforce group identities (Van Gennep, 1908/1960). Ideas of a charismatic leader may be transformed into new rules or traditions to legitimate particular shared values (Weber, 1922/1978). And religious ideas can be used to legitimate solidarity, obedience, and morale. This may include the use of emotional manipulation, such as the promise of divine bliss and the fear of punitive divine forces (Poggi, 2001; Machiavelli, 1532/2009).

Conflicts may exist between the nature of the legitimacy of different elements of organizational structure and implemented practices. Such conflicts can be resolved by means of covered operations, the elimination of information, ambiguous communications, ceremonial rather than practical activities, and by claims of the need for reorganization and trust (Powell & DiMaggio, 1991; Davenport & Leitch, 2005; Bosch, 2016).

Social influence within organizations

Social influence techniques may be used within organizations to effect the socialization of organizational members, shaping their goals, values, perspectives, attitudes, commitments, and behaviors. A first way of influencing organizational members in this sense is through the design of the formal organization. The way in which the organization is set up through units such as layers, departments, divisions, and teams can foster attachments and commitment to such units. The organization of positions and roles may influence identities. Creating formal possibilities for face-to-face encounters may help strengthen bonds and commitment (Lincoln & Kalleberg, 1990; Hardy & Clegg, 2006; Bosch, 2016).

The informal organization can also have socialization effects on organizational members. Influencing the constitution of informal groups or cohesive networks can activate group pressures leading to the internalization of desired values and norms. Organizational members can be recruited based on similarities in education, experiences, skills, and behaviors. Developing or steering an organizational culture through the development of a vision, mission, values, ethical guidelines, and supported practices such as offering long-term employment, career paths, and education may also affect values and norms, attitudes, identities, loyalty, and commitment of organizational members (Barnard, 1938/1968; Lincoln & Kalleberg, 1990; Schein, 2010; Bosch, 2016).

Reward systems may influence values and identifications. Individual rewards may support the development of independence goals and self-direction and achievement values, whereas collective rewards may support commitments to groups, units, or the organization overall. Non-financial rewards can strengthen loyalty and commitment (Lincoln & Kalleberg, 1990; Bosch, 2016).

Processes of surveillance, assessment, and discipline can have socializing effects by stimulating conformity, orderliness, punctuality, responsibility, and organizational identification and solidarity. Allowing for participation, autonomy, and employee ownership can also help organizational socialization by creating feelings of community. Organizational goals, visions, and strategies can aim to define collective purposes and processes with which organizational members can identify. These may be supported by means of symbols, organizational communications, and public speeches, the definition of enemies, and the performance of rituals or organization of social events (O'Neill, 1986; Clegg & Haugaard, 2012; Freedman, 2013; Bosch, 2016; Gómez-Mejía et al., 2016).

Another organizational social influence technique is the use of propaganda, consisting of the presentation of sets of symbols to influence opinions, beliefs, or actions. Propaganda may use various media formats including texts, audio, images, films, and other types of symbols. It may include such items as striking facts, 'fake news', stereotypes to define enemies, and the writing of alternative histories, or popular literature promoting particular ideas. It can aim to influence the image of an organization, stimulate the development of desired identities, demonstrate the desirability of products or services, or present an overarching ideology that supports existing structures of power by stimulating conformity. Propaganda can be effective when it fits the psychological needs of the intended audience and does not stray too far from widely held views among the audience (Lenski, 1966; Merton, 1968; Foucault, 1975/1977; Engelstad, 2009; Bosch, 2016).

Social influence techniques can be combined to form processes of socialization. These may become expressed in initiation processes and ceremonies, the encapsulation of members into particular groups, the provision of communal education, and the provision of role models and mentoring. Socialization in organizations may also result from behaviors when organizational members imitate others or perform organizational roles. Surveillance and disciplinary practices in organizations can stimulate self-socialization. The use of 'technologies of the self', such as confession, therapy, or self-examination may also contribute to organizational socialization (Mead, 1934/1972; Foucault, 1975/1977, 1976/1978; Bandura, 1977; Engelstad, 2009; Bosch, 2016; Clegg et al., 2019).

Developments in ICT have produced many possibilities for the application of legitimation and social influence techniques, as described in Chapter 4. Within organizations, various ICT platforms may exist that support such possibilities, but external platforms such as websites, social media platforms, blogs, and other communication channels on the internet can also be used to establish loyalties to the organization, its vision, brands, and more. ICT platforms can also stimulate particular types of identity by creating online communities with a particular focus, mode of reasoning, and emotional attraction (Clegg et al., 2019).

Limits exist to the effectiveness of legitimation and social influence techniques, due to ideas about legitimacy, values, and norms that organizational members derive from the various groups they belong to. Loyalties and commitments to other groups and organizations may exist that contradict or conflict with organizational ideas of authority, values, norms, loyalties, and commitments. Different elements of internal company policies may contradict or conflict with each other, making legitimation and social influence techniques ineffective. Actual behavior may not match espoused organizational values, leading to disenchantment among members (Bosch, 2016; Clegg et al., 2019).

Strategy within organizations

Strategies are used more or less consciously within organizations. In the development of such strategies, at least some information is collected and analyzed, and certain evaluations are made of internal structures of power, performance of (parts and members of) the organization, expectations of stakeholders, and relevant internal and external events. The power of those participating in decision-making, as well as existing procedures and interaction processes influence the development of strategies. Once at least some information has been collected and analyzed, objectives may be determined, strategic approaches may be considered, and scenarios may be drawn up. Implemented strategies can become expressed in organizational policies (Child, 1997; Hatch & Cunliffe, 2006; Bosch, 2016).

Strategic approaches may be considered to attain the objectives that were determined, including the use of various social control techniques. A strategic choice for the use of force and coercion may lead to desired adjustments in behavior, but it may also lead to resistance and negative effects on performance, and it may encourage members of the organization to deceive their supervisors. To avoid this, strategies may combine coercion with inducement. A first modality of this consists of the strategic setup of the formal and informal organization, the design of organizational roles, jobs, and the production or service provision process, and the role for innovation. Another modality of the combination of coercion and inducement is formed by strategic policies. One area of such strategic policies is constituted by employment policies. A choice may be made to provide employees with lifetime employment, which provides the strategic advantages of having employees available when they are needed, and stimulating employees to invest in organization specific training. A strategic choice for the provision of lifetime employment may also enhance trust, loyalty, commitment, and identification with the organization. Decision-making, coordination, organizational socialization, and relations with unions may be improved. Alternatively, the strategic choice may be made to use an up-or-out system. This can enhance the motivations of younger employees, but it can demotivate more senior ones. A chasm may develop between senior partners who have made it and junior employees that have to prove themselves to their seniors. A third option is the use of an in-or-out system. In such a system, employees enter at every level and may be asked to leave at any point in time on the basis of poor performance, a lack of fit, or external economic conditions. Whereas this strategic option provides flexibility in terms of size and constitution of the workforce, and limits the development or impact of unions, if so desired, it undermines relationship-based coordination, job specific training, and organizational socialization. A mixed employment system may also be chosen, with stable fulltime employment for core employees and flexible employment for others. This combines the advantages of stable employment with those of an in-and-out system, but it creates a chasm between core employees and those with flexible employment (Beer et al., 1984; Bosch, 2016; Gómez-Mejía et al., 2016).

Hiring policies may be strategically oriented at internal recruitment. This supports the development of organization specific skills, knowledge sharing, and loyalty and commitment among organizational members, but it limits flexibility. An alternative strategy is using external recruitment, which allows for the hiring of employees with special expertise, innovative ideas, or perspectives. Using both internal and external recruitment may combine advantages of both but may also lead to frustrations and turnover if employees resent recruitment decisions. Strategies for termination can aim to enhance economic performance or the fit between organizational members. Criteria that may be used include seniority and performance. The use of seniority may lead to a loss of high performing members, whereas the use of performance may create incentives for effort as well as negatively affect loyalty, commitment, and morale. An alternative is the use of early retirement which may have positive effects on performance as well as loyalty, commitment, and morale of remaining members, but which may be costly, induce high performing members to leave, and lead to discrimination complaints (Beer et al., 1984; Bosch, 2016; Gómez-Mejía et al., 2016).

Policies for promotion may strategically aim at meeting skill requirements or retaining employee commitment. Such policies can be based on relative performance or abilities, in which case performance of the overall organization may be served. But promotion policies can also be based on seniority, which supports organization-specific training and loyalty, and prevents arbitrary decisions by managers, but may undermine performance (Beer et al., 1984; Bosch, 2016; Gómez-Mejía et al., 2016).

Education policies may aim to meet skill requirements and performance, as well as to enhance motivation, loyalty, and commitment. They may be aimed at providing general or specialized knowledge. General knowledge can make organizational members widely employable which can enhance the general level of knowledge available as well as provide flexibility and a sense of community. Specialized knowledge can provide specific expertise necessary for overall performance of production or service processes. It also enhances the dependence of members on the organization. Another strategic choice in education policies is whether to aim them at individuals, teams, or other types of groups. Providing education to teams or groups can activate group learning processes that stimulate a transmission of knowledge and skills, but it can also activate group processes averse to effective learning. A strategic choice must be made between providing education on- or off-the-job. On-the-job education provides relevant practical experience and allows for the passing on of currently held skills, but it can slow down operations and experienced workers may withhold information. Off-the-job education offers the opportunity to provide more background information and new insights, but it renders control to external parties (Nonaka & Takeuchi, 1995; Bosch, 2016; Gómez-Mejía et al., 2016). Strategies in education policy may aim at improving specific competences for a particular issue, a process that has been referred to as single-loop learning. They may also aim to modify underlying goals, values, norms, beliefs, policies, and behaviors, which has been called double-loop learning (Argyris & Schön, 1978). Education policies may aim at exploitation of existing knowledge or exploration to develop knowledge (March, 1991). They may also aim to establish or support communities of practice in which knowledge is exchanged and developed (Wenger, 1998).

Reward policies can be based on individual and/or collective performance. A strategic choice for rewarding individual performance can enhance individual performance levels and the retention of high performers, but it requires an adequate measurement of individual performance. This may lead to a narrow focus on measurable indicators. It may also lead to conflict between organizational members, and it may have a discouraging effect on teamwork. When instead a strategy of team-based compensation is used, team cohesiveness and cooperation are promoted. But this may undermine individual efforts and it may lead to conflicts and claims of unfairness. It may also be difficult to adequately determine measures of team performance, which may lead to conflict between teams and a drop in performance. Yet another strategic choice is to make compensation dependent on plant- or organization-wide performance through gain or profit sharing or stock-based compensation. This can enhance plant or organizational cohesion, cooperation, and identification, and measurements may be relatively easy to make. Overall payments become dependent on overall performance, which provides financial flexibility to an organization and allows for the recruitment of top talent. But organization-wide compensation may demotivate performance of individuals and teams. And because compensation may be unstable due to dependence on overall performance, conflicts may arise. A compensation strategy can also combine individual and collective performance related pay. While this may lead to a combination of the advantages of the different approaches, it may also be difficult to determine fair and reasonable levels of individual and collective pay leading to a combination of their disadvantages. To attract new employees, the strategic choice may be made to pay efficiency wages that are above competitive wages. This allows for the recruitment of top talent and the stimulation of performance, but it may reduce overall performance due to an increase in labor costs (Bosch, 2016; Gómez-Mejía et al., 2016).

A social control strategy of divide and conquer can aim at altering internal structures of power. Downsizings or reorganizations may be used to eliminate members, functions, hierarchical levels, divisions, products, and services. They may also aim to support the formation of alliances, joint ventures, or networks with other organizations. Units can be merged or split up to enhance control, and work processes can be expanded or simplified for a similar reason. Groups such as quality control circles may be set up to break the solidarity of work groups and unions (Bosch, 2016; Gómez-Mejía et al., 2016).

A number of strategies are concerned with the way in which an organization acts toward unions. Under a union acceptance strategy, union representation of employees is seen as legitimate and collective bargaining is accepted. A union substitution strategy implies the removal of incentives for unionization by demonstrating sensitivity to the needs of employees by offering stable employment, career paths, education, and participation. In a union suppression strategy, attempts are made to prevent the formation of unions by means of delocalization, decentralization, anti-union lobbying, the undermining of union leadership, and the use of strike breakers, espionage, and propaganda (Bosch, 2016; Gómez-Mejía et al., 2016).

The choices of strategies for different policy fields may be combined into overall strategic approaches to management policies and practices. A number of ideal typical overall management strategies have been distinguished. In practice, overall strategies tend to combine different elements from the ideal typical strategies described here. A bureaucratic overall strategy uses a bureaucratic control system as described above. Bureaucratic policies include basing recruitment, promotion, and education on formal qualifications, conduct, and experience, using top-down, formal, and standardized social control techniques, and basing legitimation on the implementation of formal rules and legislations. A bureaucratic overall strategy may lead to a competent, compliant, predictable, and efficient organization as long as the environment does not change too drastically. But it may also lead to alienation and conflict (Weber, 1922/1978; Beer et al., 1984; Wallace, 1998; Bosch, 2016; Gómez-Mejía et al., 2016; Clegg et al., 2019).

An alternative overall strategy is a high commitment strategy. Such a strategy uses a corporatist control system as described above. The extensive hierarchies and formal rules entail many differences in status and responsibilities, which divides informal loyalties and enhances loyalty to the organization. Other elements include the provision of permanent employment to a core workforce, career paths based on seniority, extensive training in multiple organization-specific skills, rewards based on seniority, skills, and collective performance, and extensive benefits. All these policies aim to enhance loyalty and commitment to the organization. Organizational communication is extensive and participation of organizational members occurs through suggestion programs, problem-solving groups, and joint labor-management committees. Much importance is attached to ceremony, ritual, and symbolism which aim to evoke feelings of community in support of organizational values and norms. All these practices aim at and work to enhance commitment of the core workforce, which affects productivity, quality, and flexibility (Beer et al., 1984; Lincoln & Kalleberg, 1990; Ichniowski et al., 2000; Bosch, 2016; Gómez-Mejía et al., 2016).

Yet another possibility is the use of a market-oriented strategy. In such a strategy, management policies and practices are based on exchanges between an organization and its members. Work is broken down into concrete tasks that can be contracted out or outsourced. Organizational members are recruited to perform such tasks and they are dismissed whenever the organization sees fit. Compensation is based on merit and performance. A market-based control system is used. This market-oriented strategy stimulates task performance and leads to flexibility. It does not support commitment or loyalty to the organization, and it may lead to conflicts between competing members (Beer et al., 1984; Bosch, 2016; Gómez-Mejía et al., 2016). A specific market-oriented type of overall management strategy is an enterprising strategy in which an entrepreneurial social control system is used. Competition between groups is stirred up, while at the same time quality control and communication groups are used to support quality, coordination, legitimation, and socialization (Du Gay & Salaman, 1992). The use of ICT can support market-oriented strategies by providing intermediary platforms. This may coincide with a decentralized approach to management based on self-selection, projects, and fluidity. Where large projects are undertaken with the participation of multiple organizations and stakeholders, collaborations can be based on specific deliverables, contracts, projections, connecting ICT platforms and administrative systems, temporary project teams, scrum meetings, and strategic interaction based on relative positions of power – often implying a 'messy muddling through' emergent overall project management strategy (Clegg et al., 2017; Clegg et al., 2019).

A patronage strategy implies that authorities are linked to individuals rather than positions. In such a strategy, recruitment, career paths, and rewards are all based on personal relations. Compliance is attained through (the threat of) force and traditional and social norms, and often a patronal control system is used. Decision-making is ad hoc and depends on the individuals involved. This type of strategy is corruption prone (Norris, 2012).

A specific type of ICT-oriented strategy is that of digital transformation. This strategy aims to achieve new overall business models and strategies, as well as new or improved products and services through the use of ICT technologies in business processes and information systems. Core resources in this process are connectivity, data, and storage and processing power provided by ICT systems. The aim in digital transformation is to use these resources as a basis for developing a digital business model and strategy through an analysis of the organization's current market and internal situation, its digital potential for additional and new value chains, possibilities for implementation of digital objectives, and the planning of the required enterprise architecture. The use of flexible multifunctional teams and organizational architectures form part of a strategy that aims to be agile in light of fast changing technology. A digital transformation strategy may include the setting up of platforms, the use of data science and AI as part of business and marketing analytics, performing fast-paced digital experiments, branding, and proactive, customized, and engaged communication (Rogers, 2016; Zimmermann et al., 2021).

Once assessments have been made and strategies have been considered, more or less conscious decisions can be made as to which strategies to choose and how to implement and evaluate them. Arriving at such a decision may include such processes as meeting, suggesting, discussing, negotiating, persuading, forming coalitions, compromising, exchanging, and vetoing. Decision making is also subject to the psychological characteristics of those involved in context, as described in Chapter 3, unexpected events, and difficulties of finding required information and adequate solutions. Once decisions have been reached, responsibilities can be assigned, resources can be allocated, and implementation plans and evaluation schemes can be drawn up (Porter, 1985; Morgan, 1986; Freedman, 2013; French et al., 2015; Bosch, 2016; Barney & Hesterly, 2019; Clegg et al., 2019). Implementation of strategies can be supported by the creation of powerful supportive coalitions. Creating a sense of urgency may stimulate actions in line with strategic choices, as may supportive communications, the provision of resources, offering relevant training opportunities, and providing short-term wins. Reinforcement of implementation can be provided in the form of supportive reward policies and changes in formal organizational structures and rules (Kotter, 1996; Bosch, 2016; Cameron & Green, 2019).

The actual implementation of strategic courses of action depends on the way in which powerful members or groups in organizations interact. In addition to management and administration, a variety of stakeholders may exist with varying influence on implemented strategies, ranging from shareholders to credit providers, governmental organizations, employee representatives, suppliers, customers, and pressure groups. Pressures arising from stakeholders may affect the strategic goals that are set or that arise from strategic interaction. Such goals may vary from shareholder value and organizational expansion to the maintenance of employment and environmental, social, and governance (ESG) goals. A high level of relative ownership of shares may allow for a presence on an organizational board, which provides opportunities to influence the strategic direction of an organization through appointing and dismissing managers, articulating plans, monitoring implemented strategies, and determining reward policies. When share ownership is fragmented, shareholders can still influence organizational strategies by selling or buying shares which signals preferred strategies, by actions during shareholder meetings, and through the possibility of takeovers. In response to the latter, managers can take preventive measures by stalling shares with friendly parties, creating shares without voting rights, or implementing poison pills. Information provided to stakeholders, whether or not legally required, gives them the possibility to determine whether and how to try to influence managerial strategies. In response, management may use accounting methods that conceal specific data in aggregated data (Chew, 1997; Post et al., 2002; Hatch & Cunliffe, 2006; Pendleton & Gospel, 2013; Bosch, 2016).

Shareholders can also attempt to influence managerial behavior by means of incentive contracts that link managerial compensation to measurable performance outcomes, as suggested by agency theory (Jensen & Meckling, 1976). In practice, these types of incentive contracts may lead managers to focus narrowly on measurable indicators and poor risk projects, to the manipulation of accounting measures, timing of payments, and public announcements, and to ad hoc adjustments in compensation schemes when managerial compensation threatens to diminish. The latter may be due to information asymmetry between managers and shareholders, or to attempts to avoid litigation or bad publicity (Aguinis et al., 2018). An alternative is to focus on personal and situational factors that may help to align the interests of managers with shareholders or other stakeholders, as suggested by stewardship theory. According to this view, socially oriented motivations of, and identification with the organization by managers, support cooperative behavior toward organizational objectives. Selecting managers on the basis of the presence of these types of motivations and identifications, and providing situational support through the use of a high commitment strategy in a supportive cultural environment are seen as possibilities to achieve a coincidence of interests between stakeholders and managers. Due to its dependence on trust, this stewardship approach risks falling prey to opportunistic behavior by managers, indicating the need for a pragmatic combination with ideas from agency theory (Davis et al., 1997).

Interactions of managers with unions, where they exist, occur during bargaining processes concerned with employment conditions and policies. Such bargaining may occur at a national, regional, sector, company, plant, or employee level. Several strategic types of bargaining have been distinguished. Integrative bargaining aims at solving mutual problems, distributive bargaining at resolving conflicts of interest, and intra-organizational bargaining at achieving consensus among groups. Bargaining tends to start by parties making excessive demands which are then toned down in subsequent negotiations. To support their demands, unions may organize strikes, slowdowns, or pickets. On their side, management may resort to layoffs or lockouts, the cutting of wages, or the use of strike breakers. Threats can be made, espionage performed, and propaganda used. To resolve the situation, concessions can be made to reach a settlement, which may also entail the use of mediation or arbitration. Under governmental regulations, resulting agreements on employment conditions and policies may hold for parties not participating in the bargaining process (Strauss, 1998; Blanpain, 2014; Bosch, 2016; Gómez-Mejía et al., 2016).

Strategic interactions between organizational members have at times been described in terms of games. This includes games such as those that were discussed in Chapter 5. Mintzberg (1985) distinguished thirteen additional types of games specific to potential strategic interactions within organizations. In an insurgency game, low status members of organizations aim to resist authority, expertise, or established ideology. High status members may react by playing a counter-insurgency game. In a sponsorship game, low status members aim to attach themselves to high status members; in an alliance building game, members with similar status negotiate mutual support; and in the empire building and budgeting games, members with high status build power bases with subordinates. An expertise game implies the building of a power base on actual or pretended expertise. In a lording game, low status members aim to exercise legitimate authority over members with even lower status. Line vs. staff games occur when a rivalry exists between line managers and staff members that becomes expressed in mutual illegitimate exercises of legitimate power. When alliance or empire building games lead to two major power blocs, a zero-sum rival camps game may occur over bases of power. Strategic candidate games refer to the promotion of strategic candidates by members or groups in the organization. In a whistle blowing game, information is used by an insider to effect organizational change by exposing questionable or illegal behavior. Finally, in a Young Turks game, an attempt is made by a group close to the center of power of an organization to institute major change in terms of strategy, expertise, ideology, or leadership, while retaining the system of authority.

Digitalization strategies may aim at replacing labor by means of ICT. Data science and artificial intelligence applications and robots in different shapes and forms can be used for this purpose. Another use of ICT is the recruitment of employees from areas that are geographically remote from an organization by providing possibilities for employees to perform their work online. This enhances possibilities for organizations to use market-oriented strategies. Digital platforms and media also allow for the inclusion of views of various stakeholders in the strategy formation process, as well as the influencing of such views by organizations (Clegg et al., 2019).

Once strategies have been decided, whether or not consciously, they may be hard to change significantly because constraints exist due to existing structures of power, the valuing of traditions and the status quo, existing investments in people and technologies, and legal restrictions and other types of formal and informal rules. A significant change may therefore require a high level of dissatisfaction and models for new behavior. Providing convincing proof for a need for change, indicating opportunities for improvement, establishing consensus among leaders and top level managers, and establishing a mandate for change can support significant changes in strategy and organization. A significant change in goals, membership, or technologies may also support significant changes in strategies (Kotter, 1996; Bosch, 2016; Cameron & Green, 2019).

Collective power and empowerment

Knowledge of collective power can be highly empowering. Although collective power can be abusive to the extreme, as history so chillingly attests, it also forms the basis of our collective well-being. In light of this, it is of the utmost importance to discuss elements of collective power in a plain, systematic, comprehensive, and clear fashion. Clarifying elements of collective power this way to a wide audience empowers it to recognize and if possible, resist abusive uses of collective power while supporting constructive uses.

Epilogue

The aim of this book has been to clarify the concept of power to such an extent that it will help readers recognize, understand, and constructively use various aspects of power as they occur in their particular situations. The presented toolbox of concepts allows the selection of those elements of the concept of power that provide the most constructive and effective practical understanding in particular situations. Knowledge of such key components of the concept of power is empowering. It is empowering to learn about manifestations of structures of power, individual power, exercising power, strategy, and collective power. Understanding such conceptual components empowers those that have it to use their understanding in interpreting, theorizing about, and dealing with the complexities of power in their particular situations without being tied to any preconceived general theories about power – general theories that have so often been abused.

References

Aguinis, H., Gomez-Mejia, L.R., Martin, G.P., & Joo, H. (2018). CEO pay is indeed decoupled from CEO performance: Charting a path for the future. *Management Research, 16*(1), 117–136. https://doi.org/10.1108/MRJIAM-12-2017-0793.

Argyris, C. & Schön, D. (1978). *Organizational learning: A theory of action perspective.* Reading, MA: Addison-Wesley.

Ashforth, B. (1994). Petty tyranny in organizations. *Human Relations, 47*(7), pp. 755–778.

Bach, S. (2013). Performance management. In S. Bach & M.R. Edwards (Eds.), *Managing human resources: Human resources in transition* (5th ed.) (pp. 221–242). Chichester: John Wiley & Sons.

Bahnish, M. (2000). Embodied work, divided labour: Subjectivity and the scientific management of the body in Frederick W. Taylor's 1907 'Lecture on management'. *Body & Society, 6*(1), 51–67. https://doi.org/10.1177/1357034X00006001004.

Bandura, A. (1977). *Social learning theory.* Englewood Cliffs, NJ: Prentice-Hall.

Barbalet, J.M. (1985). Power and resistance. *The British Journal of Sociology, 36*(4), pp. 531–548. https://doi.org/10.2307/590330.

Bardon, T., Clegg, S.R., & Josserand, E. (2012). Exploring identity construction from a critical management perspective. *M@n@gement, 15*(4), 350–366. https://doi.org/10.3917/mana.154.0351.

Barker, J.R. (1993). Tightening the iron cage: Concertive control in self-managing teams. *Administrative Science Quarterly, 38*(3), 408–437. https://doi.org/10.2307/2393374.

Barnard, C.I. (1938/1968). *The functions of the executive* (13th anniversary ed.). Cambridge, MA: Harvard University Press.

Barney, J.B. & Hesterly, W.S. (2019). *Strategic management & competitive advantage* (6th ed.). New York: Pearson.

Bass, B.M. & Bass, R. (2008). *The bass handbook of leadership: Theory, research, and managerial applications* (4th ed.). New York: Free Press.

Beer, M., Spector, B., Lawrence, P.R., Mills, D.Q., & Walton, R.E. (1984). *Managing human assets*. New York: The Free Press.

Bessant, J. & Tidd, J. (2015). *Innovation and entrepreneurship* (3rd ed.). Chichester: Wiley.

Blanpain, R. (Ed.) (2014). *Comparative labour law and industrial relations in industrialized market economies* (11th ed.). Alphen aan den Rijn: Kluwer Law International.

Bosch, R. (2016). *Power: A conceptual analysis*. The Hague: Eleven International Publishing.

Cameron, E. & Green, M. (2019). *Making sense of change management: A complete guide to the models, tools and techniques of organizational change* (5th ed.). Philadephia, PA: Kogan Page.

Caramani, D. (Ed.) (2020). *Comparative politics* (5th ed.). Oxford: Oxford University Press.

Castells, M. (2009). *Communication power*. Oxford: Oxford University Press.

Castells, M. (2010). *The Information age: Economy, society, and culture. Volume I: the rise of the network society* (2nd ed.). Chichester: Wiley-Blackwell.

Central Intelligence Agency (2020). *The CIA world factbook 2020–2021*. New York: Skyhorse Publishing.

Chew, D.H. (Ed.) (1997). *Studies in international corporate finance and governance systems: A comparison of the US, Japan, & Europe*. Oxford: Oxford University Press.

Child, J. (1997). Strategic choice in the analysis of action, structure, organizations and environment: Retrospect and prospect. *Organization Studies, 18*(1), pp. 43–76. https://doi.org/10.1177/017084069701800104.

Clegg, S.R. (1989). *Frameworks of power*. London: SAGE.

Clegg, S.R. (2009). *Managing power in organizations: The hidden history of its constitution*. In S.R. Clegg & M. Haugaard (Eds.), *The SAGE handbook of power* (pp. 310–331). Los Angeles, CA: SAGE.

Clegg, S.R. & Haugaard, M. (Eds.) (2012). *Power and organizations*. Los Angeles, CA: SAGE.

Clegg, S.R., Pina e Cunha, M., Rego, A., & Dias, J. (2013). Mundane objects and the banality of evil: The sociomateriality of a death camp. *Journal of Management Inquiry, 22*(3), 325–340. https://doi.org/10.1177/1056492612461949.

Clegg, S.R., Biesenthal, C., Sankaran, S., & Pollack, J. (2017). Power and sensemaking in megaprojects. In B. Flyvbjerg (Ed.), *The Oxford handbook of megaproject management* (pp. 238–258). Oxford: Oxford University Press.

Clegg, S., Kornberger, M., Pitsis, T.S., & Mount, M. (2019). *Managing & organizations: An introduction to theory and practice* (5th ed.). Los Angeles, CA: SAGE.

Courpasson, D. (2000). Managerial strategies of domination: Power in soft bureaucracies. *Organization Studies, 21*(1), 141–161. https://doi.org/10.1177/0170840600211001.

Courpasson, D. & Clegg, S. (2006). Dissolving the iron cages? Tocqueville, Michels, bureaucracy and the perpetuation of elite power. *Organization, 13*(3), pp. 319–343. https://doi.org/10.1177/1350508406063481.

Davenport, S. & Leitch, S. (2005). Circuits of power in practice: Strategic ambiguity as delegations of authority. *Organization Studies, 26*(11), pp. 1602–1622. https://doi.org/10.1177/0170840605054627.

Davis, J.H., Schoorman, F.D., & Donaldson, L. (1997). Toward a stewardship theory of management. *Academy of Management Review, 22*(1), 20–47. https://doi.org/10.2307/259223.

Du Gay, P. & Salaman, G. (1992). The cult[ure] of the customer. *Journal of Management Studies, 19*(5), pp. 615–633. https://doi.org/10.1111/j.1467-6486.1992.tb00681.x.

Engelstad, F. (2009). Culture and power. In S.R. Clegg & M. Haugaard (Eds.), *The SAGE handbook of power* (pp. 210–238). Thousand Oaks, CA: SAGE.

Ferlie, E., & Pettigrew, A. (1996/1998). Managing through networks. In C. Mabey, G. Salaman, & J. Storey (Eds.), *Strategic human resource management: A reader* (pp. 200–222). London: SAGE.

Foucault, M. (1975/1977). *Discipline and punish: The birth of the prison* (A. Sheridan, Trans.). New York: Random House.

Foucault, M. (1976/1978). *The history of sexuality, Vol. 1: an introduction* (R. Hurley, Trans.). New York: Vintage.

Foucault, M. (1980). *Power/knowledge: Selected interviews and other writings 1972–1977* (C. Gordon, Ed. & C. Gordon, L. Marshall, J. Mepham, & K. Soper, Trans.). New York: Pantheon Books.

Freedman, L. (2013). *Strategy: A history.* Oxford: Oxford University Press.

Freeman, R.E., Harrison, J.S., Wicks, A.C., Parmar, B.L., & De Colle, S. (2010). *Stakeholder theory: The state of the art.* Cambridge: Cambridge University Press.

French, R., Rayner, C., Rees, G., Rumbles, S., Schermerhorn Jr., J., Hunt, J., & Osborn, R. (2015). *Organizational behaviour.* Chichester: Wiley.

Garfinkel, H. (1967). *Studies in ethnomethodology.* Englewood Cliffs, NJ: Prentice Hall.

Geertz, C. (1973). *The interpretation of cultures: Selected essays by Clifford Geertz.* New York: Basic Books.

Goffman, E. (1959). *The presentation of self in everyday life.* Garden City, NY: Doubleday.

Gómez-Mejía, L.R., Balkin, D.B., & Cardy, R.L. (2016). *Managing human resources* (8th ed.). Boston, MA: Pearson.

Gordon, R. (2002). Conceptualizing leadership with respect to its historical–contextual antecedent to power. *The Leadership Quarterly, 13*(2), 151–167. https://doi.org/10.1016/S1048-9843(02)00095-4.

Gramsci, A. (1971). *Selections from the prison notebooks* (Q. Hoare & G.N. Smith, Trans.). New York: International Publishers.

Greifeneder, R., Jaffé, M.E., Newman, E.J., & Schwarz, N. (2021). What is new and true about fake news? In R. Greifeneder, M.E. Jaffé, E.J. Newman, N. & Schwarz (2021) (Eds.). *The psychology of fake news: Accepting, sharing, and correcting misinformation* (pp. 1–8). London: Routledge.

Grusky, D.B., Ku, M.C., & Szelényi, S. (Eds.) (2008). *Social stratification: Class, race, and gender in sociological perspective* (3rd ed.). Boulder, CO: Westview Press.

Hall, P.A. & Soskice, D. (Eds.) (2001). *Varieties of capitalism: The institutional foundations of comparative advantage.* Oxford: Oxford University Press.

Hardy, C. & Clegg, S. (2006). Some dare call it power. In S.R. Clegg, C. Hardy, W. Nord, & T. Lawrence (Eds.), *The SAGE handbook of organization studies* (2nd ed.) (pp. 754–775). London: SAGE.

Hardy, C., Palmer, I., & Phillips, N. (2000). Discourse as a strategic resource. *Human Relations, 53*(9), pp. 1227–1247. https://doi.org/10.1177/0018726700539006.

Haslam, S.A., Reicher, S.D., & Platow, M.J. (2011). *The New psychology of leadership: Identity, influence and power.* New York: Psychology Press.

Hatch, M.J. & Cunliffe, A.L. (2006). *Organization theory* (2nd ed.). Oxford: Oxford University Press.

Hirschman, A.O. (1970). *Exit, voice, and loyalty: Responses to decline in firms, organizations, and states.* Cambridge, MA: Harvard University Press.

Hofstede, G., Hofstede, G.J., & Minkov, M. (2010). *Cultures and organizations: Software of the mind. Intercultural cooperation and its importance for survival* (rev. & exp. 3rd ed.). New York: McGraw-Hill.

Ichniowski, C., Levine, D.I., Olson, C., & Strauss, G. (Eds.) (2000). *The American workplace: Skills, compensation, and employee involvement.* Cambridge: Cambridge University Press.

Inglehart, R.F. (2018). *Cultural evolution: People's motivations are changing and reshaping the world.* Cambridge: Cambridge University Press.

Jensen, M.C. & Meckling, W.H. (1976). Theory of the firm: Managerial behavior, agency costs, and ownership structure. *Journal of financial economics*, *3*(4), 305–360. https://doi.org/10.1016/0304-405X(76)90026-X.

Kanter, R.M. (1988). When a thousand flowers bloom: Structural, collective, and social conditions for innovation in organizations. *Research in Organizational Behavior*, *10*, 169–211.

Keister, L.A. & Southgate, D.E. (2012). *Inequality: A contemporary approach to race, class, and gender*. Cambridge: Cambridge University Press.

Kochan, T. & Osterman, P. (1994/1998). The mutual gains enterprise. In C. Mabey, G. Salaman, & J. Storey (Eds.), *Strategic human resource management: A reader* (pp. 223–236). London: SAGE.

Kotter, J.P. (1996). *Leading change*. Boston, MA: Harvard Business School Press.

Kotter, J.P. (1990/1998). What leaders really do. In *Harvard Business Review on leadership* (pp. 37–60). Boston, MA: Harvard Business School Publishing.

Lansford, T. (Ed.) (2019). *Political handbook of the world 2018–2019*. Los Angeles, CA: CQ Press.

Lenski, G. (1966). *Power and privilege: A theory of social stratification*. New York: McGraw-Hill.

Lincoln, J.R. & Kalleberg, A.L. (1990). *Culture, control, and commitment: A study of work organization and work attitudes in the United States and Japan*. Cambridge: Cambridge University Press.

Machiavelli, N. (1532/2009). *The prince* (T. Parks, Trans.). London: Penguin Books.

March, J.G. (1991). Exploration and exploitation in organizational learning. *Organization Science*, *2*(1), 71–87. https://doi.org/10.1287/orsc.2.1.71.

McGregor, D. (1960). *The human side of enterprise*. New York: McGraw-Hill.

Mead, G.H. (1934/1972). *Mind, self, and society: From the standpoint of a social behaviorist* (C.W. Morris, Ed., Intr.). Chicago, IL: The University of Chicago Press.

Merton, R.K. (1968). *Social theory and social structure* (enlarged ed.). New York: The Free Press.

Mintzberg, H. (1983). *Structure in fives: Designing effective organizations*. Englewood Cliffs, NJ: Prentice-Hall.

Mintzberg, H. (1985). The organization as political arena. *Journal of Management Studies*, *22*(2), pp. 133–154. https://doi.org/10.1111/j.1467-6486.1985.tb00069.x

Morgan, G. (1986). *Images of organization*. Thousand Oaks, CA: SAGE.

Mumby, D.K. (2004). Discourse, power, and ideology: Unpacking the critical approach. In D. Grant, C. Hardy, C. Oswick, & L.L. Putnam (Eds.), *The SAGE handbook of organizational discourse* (pp. 237–258). London: SAGE.

Nonaka, I. & Takeuchi, H. (1995). *The knowledge-creating company: How Japanese companies create the dynamics of innovation*. Oxford: Oxford University Press.

Norris, P. (2012). *Making democratic governance work: How regimes shape prosperity, welfare, and peace*. Cambridge: Cambridge University Press.

O'Neill, J. (1986). The disciplinary society: From Weber to Foucault. *British Journal of Sociology*, *37*(1), pp. 42–60. https://doi.org/10.2307/591050.

Pendleton, A. & Gospel, H. (2013). Corporate governance and human resource management. In S. Bach & M.R. Edwards (Eds.), *Managing human resources: Human resources in transition* (5th ed.) (pp. 61–78). Chichester: John Wiley & Sons.

Poggi, G. (2001). *Forms of power*. Cambridge: Polity.

Porter, M.E. (1985). *Competitive advantage: Creating and sustaining superior performance*. New York: The Free Press.

Porter, M.E. (1998). Clusters and the new economics of competition. *Harvard Business Review*, November–December, 77–90.

Post, J.E., Preston, L.D., & Sachs, S. (2002). *Redefining the corporation: Stakeholder management and organizational wealth.* Stanford, CA: Stanford University Press.

Powell, W.W. & DiMaggio, P.J. (Eds.) (1991). *The new institutionalism in organizational analysis.* Chicago, IL: The University of Chicago Press.

Randall, J. & Sim, A.J. (2014). *Managing people at work.* New York: Routledge.

Robbins, S.P. & Judge, T.A. (2018). *Essentials of organizational behavior* (global 14th ed.). Harlow: Pearson.

Rogers, D.L. (2016). *The digital transformation playbook: Rethinking your business for the digital age.* New York: Columbia Business School Press.

Ros, M., Schwartz, S.H., & Surkiss, S. (1999). Basic individual values, work values, and the meaning of work. *Applied Psychology: An International Review, 48*(1), 49–71. https://doi.org/10.1111/j.1464-0597.1999.tb00048.x.

Schein, E.H. (1988). *Organizational psychology* (3rd ed.). Englewood Cliffs, NJ: Prentice-Hall.

Schein, E.H. (2010). *Organizational culture and leadership* (4th ed.). San Francisco, CA: Jossey-Bass.

Schwartz, S.H. (2007). Value orientations: Measurement, antecedents and consequences across nations. In R. Jowell, C. Roberts, R. Fitzgerald, & G. Eva (Eds.), *Measuring attitudes cross-nationally: Lessons from the European Social Survey* (pp. 169–203). London: SAGE.

Schwartz, S.H., Cieciuch, J., Vecchione, M., Davidov, E., Fischer, R., Beierlein, C., Ramos, A., Verkasalo, M.V., Lönnqvist, J.-E., Demirutku, K., Dirilen-Gumus, O., & Konty, M. (2012). Refining the theory of basic individual values. *Journal of Personality and Social Psychology, 103*(4), 663–688. https://doi.org/10.1037/a0029393.

Scott, J. (Ed.) (1994). *Power: Critical concepts.* London: Routledge.

Selznick, P. (1957). *Leadership in administration: A sociological interpretation.* New York: Harper & Row.

Sewell, G. (1998). The discipline of teams: The control of team-based industrial work through electronic and peer surveillance. *Administrative Science Quarterly, 43*(20), pp. 397–428. https://doi.org/10.2307/2393857.

Sewell, G. (2021). *Surveillance: A key idea for business and society.* London: Routledge.

Simpson, A.V., Clegg, S., & Pitsis, T. (2014). "I used to care but things have changed": A genealogy of compassion in organizational theory. *Journal of Management Inquiry, 23*(4), 347–359.

Sinclair, B. (2012). *The social citizen: Peer networks and political behavior.* Chicago, IL: The University of Chicago Press.

Smith-Doerr, L. & Powell, W.P. (2005). Networks and economic life. In N.J. Smelser & R. Swedberg (Eds.), *The handbook of economic sociology* (2nd ed.) (pp. 379–402). Princeton, NJ: Princeton University Press.

Stevenson, W.J. (2021). *Operations management* (14th ed.). New York: McGraw-Hill.

Strauss, G. (1998). Collective bargaining. In M. Poole & M. Warner (Eds.), *The IEBM handbook of human resource management* (pp. 665–676). London: International Thomson Business Press.

Taylor, F.W. (1911/1947). *Scientific management.* Westport, CT: Greenwood Press.

Van de Ven, A.H. & Hargrave, T.J. (2004). Social, technical, and institutional change: A literature review and synthesis. In M.S. Poole & A.H. Van de Ven (Eds.), *Handbook of organizational change and innovation* (pp. 259–303). Oxford: Oxford University Press.

Van Gennep, A. (1908/1960). *The rites of passage* (M.B. Vizedom & G.L. Caffee, Trans.). Chicago, IL: The University of Chicago Press.

Wallace, T. (1998). Fordism. In M. Poole & M. Warner (Eds.), *The IEMB handbook of human resource management* (pp. 363–374). London: International Thomson Business Press.

Weber, M. (1922). *GesammelteAufsätzezurWissenschaftslehre*. Tübingen: Verlag von J.C.B. Mohr (Paul Siebeck).

Weber, M. (1922/1978). *Economy and society* (G. Roth & C. Wittich, Eds.). Berkeley, CA: University of California Press.

Weick, K.E. (1995). *Sensemaking in organizations*. Thousand Oaks, CA: SAGE.

Wenger, E. (1998). *Communities of practice: Learning, meaning, and identity*. New York: Cambridge University Press.

West, D.M. (2018). *The future of work: Robots, AI, and automation*. Washington, DC: Brookings Institution Press.

Wilkinson, A., Dundon, T., & Marchington, M. (2013). Employee involvement and voice. In S. Bach & M.R. Edwards (Eds.), *Managing human resources: Human resources in transition* (5th ed.) (pp. 61–78). Chichester: John Wiley & Sons.

Winseck, D. (2019). Internet infrastructure and the persistent myth of U.S. hegemony. In B. Haggart, K. Henne, & N. Tusikov (Eds.), *Information, technology and control in a changing world: Understanding power structures in the 21st century* (pp. 93–120). Cham: Palgrave Macmillan.

Womack, J.P., Jones, D.T., & Roos, D. (1990). *The machine that changed the world*. New York: Rawson Associates.

Zimmermann, A., Schmidt, R., & Jain, L.C. (Eds.) (2021). *Architecting the digital transformation: Digital business, technology, decision support, management*. Cham: Springer.

INDEX